LAST TRAIN TO BERLIN

Hans Peter Marland

MINERVA PRESS
MONTREUX LONDON WASHINGTON

LAST TRAIN TO BERLIN
Copyright © Hans Peter Marland 1995

ISBN 1 85863 840 2

First Published 1995 by
MINERVA PRESS
1 Cromwell Place
London SW7 2JE

Printed in Great Britain by
Antony Rowe Ltd., Chippenham, Wiltshire

LAST TRAIN TO BERLIN

U.S.S.R.

MOSCOW
PODOLSK
YAVAS
TULA
USLOVAYA
STALINOGOIRSK

POLAND

BERLIN
FRANKFURT
BREST
KURSK

PRAGUE
OLOMUCE
TABOR
CZECHOSLOVAKIA
BRUNO

ROMANIA
ODESSA
KRONSTADT
POCSANI
PLOIESTI
CONSTANTA

------ 1945
--·--·-- 1946 - 1949
--··--··-- REPATRIATION DEC. 49

CONTENTS

INTRODUCTION

On the day the Second World War ended in 1945 the writer, a German Army officer, hoped to surrender with the men under his command to nearby American forces. Instead they were forced to join the thousands rounded up by the Red Army.

He did not get back home from the Soviet Union for nearly five years.

This is an account of his experiences during that time.

AND STALIN SAID

I told Stalin that Britain was short of coal.

Stalin replied, "Then use German prisoners in the mines; that is what I am doing."

From *The Second World War* Vol. VI, page 581 by Winston Churchill.

July 25, 1945

FOREWORD

Four and a half years after the end of the 1939-45 conflict, I finally made it home, on the very last train carrying prisoners of war released by the Soviet Union.

No one in their right mind would have volunteered to spend all that time deep inside Russia, but there was a good side to the experience: the fellowship of other PoWs will live in my mind until I die. I shall also carry with me insights into the staunch Soviet citizens who depended so greatly on us to provide the pick-and-shovel labour during that time when Russia was desperately short of manpower.

Those days sharpened my sense of humour. Consequently, I may seem to skate over the severity of the conditions under which we lived and worked. All we could do, after all, was make the best of the situation and live each day as it happened. Some events were downright hilarious and may appear barely credible, but everything about which I write actually happened.

I wish to dedicate this account to the memory of Heinz and Wilfried, my two best friends throughout those years, but who sadly died a few years ago. With them I shared joy and sorrow and such few possessions as we had in common. They gave of their time and help whenever called upon, with no thought of thanks. In being there when the three of us needed mutual support, they live in my memory.

Though the experience taught me much about myself, particularly how to survive in difficult situations, I really could have done without it.

AN OFFICER IN PEACETIME

Three months before the War ended in 1945, I waved farewell to my mother and father until the train swung on to the main track and they were no longer in view. They walked back along the platform of Berlin's Ostbahnhof while I and the other German Army officers and men on board took the long journey to Prague to join the theatre of war in Czechoslovakia.

I was to carry in my mind's eye for the next five years a picture of my father in a brown tweed herringbone coat and his beloved tattered hat with the sweat marks around the band, and of my darling mother in her camel coat with the huge red fox collar. I remembered that her hair had swayed gently in the draught as the departing train moved past her.

It was February 1945. Having been in the army since the outbreak of war, and being descended from a line of military men, I knew there was precious little glamour in being shot at by the enemy. But I had been trained to make the best of it, so like everyone else on the train, I feared the worst and hoped for the best.

Like troops everywhere, my Company had a mascot. In our case it was a chocolate-brown pointer called Sepp which made its home with us quite happily when times were comparatively quiet. He would make his bed wherever he could away from the rain or snow, but never so far away that he couldn't keep an eye on us. One day he took a nap under one of the field guns which had not been in action for a while, but he took off like a flash of greased lightning when, without asking for his consent, someone rammed a shell into the breach and let fly. We never saw him again.

Not long after this I acquired a Welsh terrier to keep me company and we quickly established a mutual bond of love and trust. Wherever I went, Whisky went. He put up with shellfire provided he was near me. He tolerated the scrappy food. In many ways, of course, he had it easy.

For us it was a particularly nerve-wracking time, made doubly bad by seeing all around us men deserting in ever-increasing numbers. As April drew to a close it was obvious that everything was collapsing. By then there was a steady westward stream of troops hoping to reach American lines and, frankly, it was hard to blame them. We, who continued to man our posts, became steadily more anxious and it was unbelievably sweet to pick up, quite by chance, a plain language message in Morse code during the night of 8th May.

It was a short, pithy message. "Armistice. Without heavy weapons proceed to Budweis. Join Division there. CO."

At last, the war was over. Although the Allies were the victors, my main thought was one of relief that the whole sorry business had come to an end. I had survived. Soon I would be a civilian once again.

We were close to Olmütz (Olomuc) in Eastern Bohemia when we picked up the Morse code message. It had once been a major industrial town, but now it was almost totally ruined. Our advised destination, however, was a long way away, deep behind the advancing Russian forces. I felt it would be madness to go through the Russian lines, so I decided to call it a day and head for the West.

I decided to order the destruction of all our weapons, dismiss my unit and leave it to the troops to find their own individual ways to the Americans, who were known to be approaching Czechoslovakia from the west.

The following morning broke early, full of promise with a lovely pale blue sky and bright sunshine. Not knowing what lay ahead, I decided to forgo my smart officer's dress of tunic and breeches in favour of the more comfortable standard tank uniform. Instead of my shiny black leather riding boots, I put on a pair of ski boots which I felt were likely to be more suitable for the very uncertain future. Something told me to hang on to my Walther PPK pistol in case of trouble. I felt that it would be wise not to carry it in full view. As it was basically smooth on both sides, I dropped it into the bottom of my left boot so I would actually be walking on it.

In the unaccustomed quiet of that first morning of peace, one could hear the birds singing high into the sky, but for us it was a false dawn. As we would find out all too soon, there would be no joy for us that day.

We broke up into small groups. I gathered my officers, took charge of a Volkswagen Kübel (Germany's answer to the Jeep), filled it with petrol and provisions to last for several days, and headed off towards Prague and freedom. However, no sooner had we got under way than a Russian Rata fighter plane swooped down and made it very clear indeed that so far as he was concerned we were going the wrong way. His job, obviously, was to shepherd us toward the east whereas our goal was right in the opposite direction. We might have stood a chance of getting our own way with any modicum of luck, but at the very moment when we tried to outmanoeuvre the fighter plane and dash for cover in the nearby woods, our transport broke down.

There was no alternative but to leave the car stranded in the middle of a field. We felt pretty exposed as we stood around trying to decide what to keep and what to abandon, so we made quick work of packing rucksacks with anything that would obviously be useful. It was with these pathetically small collections of food and clothes that we got off that field as fast as we could and struck out towards the woods.

With any luck we should be able to escape detection, I thought, without realising that my faithful Whisky might be the one to give the game away. He stuck to my side as good as gold as we made our way over the fields, but always on the alert for danger. While we were hidden in the long grass taking a short rest, a paramilitary Czech patrol came by and Whisky rushed out to attack, barking furiously and waving his tail. I was certain this show of bravado would give away our position, and sure enough, the patrol looked around to see where Whisky had come from. Even though we were so close to them, they could not see us and quickly came to the conclusion that little Whisky was an orphan. Much to our relief, one of the group decided to adopt him, picked him up and fell into line as they went on their way.

I hated to see little Whisky carried off like that, though at least it resolved the situation. Clearly that brave little dog, sooner or later, would have given away our presence, yet I doubt if I would have had the heart to chase him away. Knowing how much I truly loved him, he probably would not have left, anyway. The alternative was unthinkable.

We carried on steadily north-west relying on ordnance survey maps and my hand-held compass. The heavy going made us tired and hungry, so when we came across a small wood with a stream running through it we settled down right by the stream, stuck our tired feet into the cool water and recovered our strength. We felt on top of the world. Not a sound, apart from the babbling water and the song of birds. Peace at last.

Very quietly, a tall civilian armed with a 98 carbine rifle appeared out of the bushes. He was smartly dressed in breeches and riding boots, and a white shirt with rolled up sleeves. His blond hair was well groomed and his keen blue eyes were those of a hunter. He was clearly as startled to see our small group as we were to be taken unawares by him.

What should I do – dig down into my ski boot and shoot him with my pistol or try to be friendly? There had been quite enough shooting all round during the past six years and the war was over, so I opted for a spot of diplomacy. Fortunately he seemed to have the same idea. He came over to the stream and settled down by our side with the carbine between his knees and lit a cigarette.

In fluent German he explained that he was in no way hostile towards us and only carried his rifle to protect his family and himself from marauding Russians. He had seen what suffering had been caused by those liberators from the east during the short time they had occupied most of Czechoslovakia and, quite simply, he told us he hated their guts.

"I just want to warn you," he said. "Do not try to get to Prague. Russian troops are everywhere. They shoot at anyone who is not marching down the main roads, whether they are in uniform or not. My advice is that you join all the other German soldiers at the earliest opportunity and walk with them in whatever direction the Russians point. The war is over; you lost and you might as well give in. Possibly this will save your lives."

He stubbed out the cigarette, wished us well, and quietly re-entered the wall of trees behind us.

Refreshed from our break, though pretty worried by what we had learned, we pushed on carefully through the wood until we came to the edge. In front of us lay a main road along which everyone was travelling in the same direction. One side was clogged with thousands of troops walking, shuffling like sheep, while the other was being used by Russian troops on horseback or riding on horse-drawn wagons. The Russians were waving their automatics and singing patriotic songs and paid scant attention to the defeated army they were steadily overhauling.

"Woyna kaput. Scoro damoy!" they would shout from time to time at the slow-moving stream of grey-uniformed troops.

Only much later did we learn to understand the Russian way of distinguishing between the various time-related expressions.

"Si chass." Now, immediate. In reality anything between this very moment and 'one day'.

"Scoro." Soon, meaning just that. Perhaps two or three weeks, or longer.

"Budit." Will be, say, in a year or two.

"Scoro budit." Will be soon. Almost certainly never, unless circumstances change.

Even with our limited knowledge of Russian we knew they were saying, "The war is over. You will be home soon". As I stood watching the spectacle, I certainly hoped they were right. Judging by the direction in which they were heading, we almost believed them. Everyone was moving west and that's where the Americans were supposed to be. So we joined the crowd and took our first steps on an eight thousand kilometre detour that was to take four years and seven months.

Had we known then, that the Western Allies and Russia had cooked up a deal on the 'peaceful' employment of German forces, things would have been very different. At that crucial time, when we stepped out of the forest and joined the great parade, we were totally unaware they had agreed that everyone who had fought the Russians was to be detained by them. It later transpired that even those who made it safely to the American lines were to be handed over.

As it was, we fell in with the hundreds of thousands of German soldiers, plodding along under a scorching hot sun. They were not only hot, but tired and disillusioned and thirsty. Food they could do without for a while longer, but they longed for a drink.

The day went on and we became ever more thirsty. Czech civilians barred us from using water taps, fountains or wells. Because we had slowed right down, the mass of humanity frequently bunched up into a mass whereupon the Red Army troops pushed us back into some semblance of order down our own side of the road, clearing the way for the Russian transport. Unlike us, they preferred horses to motor engines for pulling wagons. Their thinking was that horse fuel was less of a problem, maintenance was nil and, when it had served its usefulness, a horse could be turned into nourishing food for the troops.

Tired though we were, we kept moving because our adrenaline was still pumping. We all wanted to get as far to the west as we possibly could, hoping that somehow we would find a way to escape. At nightfall an army lorry joined us. It was being driven by a German soldier who had room for a few more. We climbed aboard and sat back and went happily on our way without being stopped.

One of the party spoke Russian and he suggested that we pull over to the left and join the Russian army as part of their column. This worked like a charm. Now and again we were questioned, but each time our linguist got us out of trouble by claiming that we belonged to the 'Freies Deutschland Division' (Free German Division) under the command of Field Marshal Paulus, the defender of Stalingrad. It was true that Paulus had set up such a division in the Soviet Union, but it had never left the PoW camp near Moscow and was never allowed to bear arms. The people who stopped us did not know this, though. After all, who else but a legitimate anti-fascist would ride amidst the might of the Red Army in an endless parade of artillery pieces, rocket launchers, personnel carriers and armour?

We continued at a fair speed and before long, came to the River Vlatava (Moldau). This time we were stopped by a Russian major who listened politely to Lt. Klein's explanations but did not believe a single word. Instead he expressed absolute astonishment at our insolence, asked us civilly to pull up on the side of the road, get off the lorry, and join the grey fellows heading back the other way.

So we were not to get to the west. After our first eighteen hours of peace we were utterly exhausted so, instead of joining the main party of German troops, we slipped off into a field and lay down in the grass. No one seemed to mind, and within minutes we were all sound asleep.

Next morning I realised it would be politic to have as few embarrassing items about my person as possible. I removed the pistol from my ski boot, dismantled it and threw the pieces as far as I could in different directions. Strangely I felt relieved that the last piece of shootable property of the German Army had gone.

Truth to tell, some weeks earlier and in anticipation of the collapse of the Third Reich, I had put together an escape package which included my packed rucksack. It was then I had decided that, if walking was to become the order of the day, it would be advisable to discard the riding boots and change into my ski boots. In those days ski boots were still made of leather, pliable and comfortable. How wise this decision had been was demonstrated very soon after we were set on the road to paradise.

Toiling along with the former German Army, it was nothing to see Red Army soldiers pull high boots from their unlucky wearer in exchange for their own army regulation footwear, no matter whether the size was correct or not. One saw up, and down the road, Russian troops sitting on the verge exchanging riding boots to get a pair of the correct size while, on our side of the road, German soldiers tried to swap Russian army boots to find a pair that fitted not too badly. In the end everyone was reasonably satisfied.

All this took time, of course, and it was common to see Russians running up the road to rejoin their units. We were not a bit bothered about how long it took for the German recipients of Russian boots to find a fit.

As with boots, so with watches. Many a wristwatch changed hands, which gave rise to the conundrum: "How can you find the direction in a pitch-dark night if you don't have a compass?"
Answer: "Take off your wristwatch, lay it on the palm of your hand and turn full circle. Your watch always disappears to the east."

I had taken care to fill my rucksack with practical things only, so I was carrying a blanket, underwear and, most important of all, spare socks. I also had a set of cutlery, writing gear, paper, string, needle and thread, a pair of scissors, a ten centimetre long nail and a box of matches.

In the Army we had been told that the last three items were the most important utensils in a soldier's pocket. A nail can be used to open things, close things, pin something to a wall, poke a hole and, if the occasion demanded, kill an opponent. With string, one can tie things up, string things up, string oneself (or others) up, and make a trap. Furthermore, string can be used as a trip wire if connected to a detonator and gelignite. The box generally supplied for matches can be used as tinder when lighting a fire. Or, being exactly one centimetre high, two centimetres wide and five centimetres long, it can double as a ruler or measuring tool. With a matchbox, therefore, one can measure the width of a road with patience and spare time.

My rucksack also contained my Leica photo camera and some film, a valuable item, which I hoped to be able to keep.

Early on the enforced march, I noticed that some of our comrades were frisked by Russian soldiers and had to stand behind their belongings which were searched for worthwhile loot. Sooner or later this was going to happen to me, but I decided it was worth trying to foil their efforts by a little camouflage.

Right across the back of my rucksack was an inside pocket, which might be made into a mini-safe. I cut off the buttons, pushed the flap inside and by stitching very accurately along the existing line of the seam, made it look as though there had never been a pocket.

The idea worked like a charm every time we were frisked, either on the roadside or, particularly, whenever we entered a detention camp. The trick was to appear to be helpful, empty the rucksack in front of the searcher and, gripping the heavy items in the pouch from the outside of the rucksack, turn it inside out and demonstrate that the sack was empty. It worked every time.

After three days of marching like lemmings and sleeping 'rough' at night, we got into a mind-numbing routine, neither knowing nor caring overmuch what lay ahead of us. The sunny weather was holding, though it was almost too hot for our liking during the day, with very warm nights. On the fourth day the weather changed with a vengeance. The heavens opened, turning the mud to treacle and soaking our heavy uniforms until they clung to our tormented bodies like floor cloths.

This was the day, too, when our captors decided to put some order into the chaos. Picture the scene: a few hundred thousand PoWs, all heading in the same direction though on different, almost parallel, routes. The march was stopped and we were made to line up in ranks of five.

A Russian sergeant – who, we soon discovered, could count five in a row and up to ten ranks – walked along the front, counting always ten ranks. After every fifty bodies he entered a mark on his note pad and placed a sentry in position. By counting the number of sentries he knew how many prisoners came under this command. One thousand PoWs made up one block.

In time, we discovered that on the same day the entire German Army taken prisoner by the Russians was divided into blocks of one thousand officers and men. Each block of men was to remain together, right through to repatriation four and a half years later.

Establishing a large gap and placing one guard at the rear and one at the front, he called the officers to the front. All twenty-seven of us marched out expecting the worst, but there appeared to be no reason other than that the officer in charge had simply wanted us to be separated from the other ranks. Senior among us was a colonel. He was a funny sort of chap, only 155cm (5ft 2in) tall, with a face the colour and texture of pigskin and a nose which resembled a shrivelled carrot. He also had a pair of piercing black eyes. His head was disproportionately large for his body.

No doubt because they were obviously so small, he was still in possession of his riding boots, whose tips turned up like the front ends of skis.

He had a croak of a voice and a twang of a Bavarian accent, not unlike the dry hinges of an old barn door. We christened him at once 'Wurzelzwerg', a name that is hard to translate precisely into English, though the closest might be 'Root Gnome'.

Wurzelzwerg held the position of PoW commanding officer right up to the time we entered our first proper camp in Mordvinia, when he was sent home because of ill health. The appointment was made by the Russians, who then had someone to have a go at and to relay their instructions. In all other respects, this poor man was completely ineffectual.

Once the nine hundred and seventy-three troops and twenty-seven officers were divided off as a block, we marched off for our fourth day of peace, still without food of any kind. The provisions my own small detachment had brought along were almost exhausted and we wondered how much longer we could carry on.

After some time we came to a road block and were made to surrender our paybooks. This was itself a soul-destroying move, for to any soldier anywhere his paybook is his passport. Without the comfort of having it in his pocket he feels like a non-person. No one told us why our paybooks had been confiscated and it was quite some time before we found out, in the course of several interrogations, that these had been garnered by the Soviet Army and kept in a huge bundle as the key to our entire block. Miraculously, they were to turn up in our camp in due course, to form the basis of our personal files.

Forty-eight years on, I am amazed that I can recall those earliest days of captivity with absolute clarity. The human brain truly keeps track of every experience, which can be brought to the fore either by concentration or by a simple jogging of the memory. By huddling over 'THE TIMES ATLAS OF THE WORLD' and studying the map of Czechoslovakia to trace the route which I took during the first days of captivity, the whole story unfolds again. Details emerge which I thought completely forgotten, such as life with the 'Wurzelzwerg'.

So, to go back: that night, the weather got worse. Rain was sluicing down and drenched our clothing right through to the skin. No one, not even our guards, found it very amusing, so we were turned into a field to settle down. Talk about leaping from the frying pan into the fire! The rain we were hoping to avoid had turned the ground into pure mud. For some reason, we were not allowed to stand, but had to lie down in rows, with no other protection than our coats. Very few of us had rain gear and only the former motorcycle riders, in their long protective rubberised coats, were reasonably comfortable.

That was some night to remember: no sleep, shivering from the wet, cold, and desperately hungry. What a miserable bunch the German Army had become. I recall that while one could not do much more than pray for a let-up in the weather, my mind's eye took me back in flashes to the brilliant sun over Greece shining out of a cloudless blue sky. To make the pangs of hunger even worse, I saw delicious meals enjoyed before the bombs tore apart the social life of Berlin, served on white damask table linen, with Rhine wine drunk from cut-glass goblets. And all the while, around and beneath, was the cold, slimy mud.

Dawn came to disturb a shallow sleep of exhaustion, and we were herded back on to the road. Miracle of miracles, the rain eased, so despite being wet through to the skin, we were able to walk and build up a certain amount of body warmth. After only a few kilometres, we turned into a large courtyard dominated by a beautiful chateau-like mansion, flanked by outbuildings and stables. Judging by the architecture and quality of construction, the place must have dated from the early eighteenth century. It was completely deserted.

Told to go inside and settle down where we wanted, I headed with my own small group of fellow travellers to the main entrance, and right up to the top floor. We opened the massive main doors and stood aghast. Beautiful furniture lay everywhere, display cabinets were untouched, and in some rooms stood crates absolutely full of delicate glassware, goblets and dishes. Wherever we looked were signs that these treasures were still being packed for safe-keeping when the owners fled from the advancing Russian Army. This house full of treasures had been left to the mercy of whoever took it over. Here was style to be enjoyed and appreciated. We might only have well water, but we most certainly would drink it from Bohemian or French crystal. We made ourselves as comfortable as possible. When again might we be invited to dine in luxury and splendour?

While we were waiting for things to develop, a field kitchen and some lorries loaded with bread arrived, and we quickly lined up to collect our feast of a ration: sauerkraut soup, kasha and a piece of bread. Kasha is a sort of porridge, made from oats, buckwheat or the like, and cooked until it is as stiff as wallpaper paste. Kasha is filling and has some nourishment, but it is utterly tasteless. For centuries entire Russian tribes had been brought up on the stuff and we all know how strong they grew. So, we thought, it might even do something for the rotten Germans. Just as well, for it was to become the most common component of any meal throughout our stay in the Soviet Union.

Let me digress. Sometimes we would get cabbage soup with fish, eyes and all, or cabbage soup without fish but with green tomatoes, or cabbage soup with fish eyes and well cooked bones. All would be served either plain, or mixed with sauerkraut. Sometimes there would be salt, a real delicacy. Later on, however, this changed slightly for the better when we officers received some sugar, fat (even fifty grammes of butter and margarine a month) and tobacco (Russian machorka). But this was months later, and only after we came under the patronage of the political forces.

I was always hungry, but unlike most people I was able to do something about it. Luckily I had brought with me a small pair of scissors. With these I was able to earn some extra food by applying my 'talents' as a hairdresser. I set up shop as a hair stylist. My first results were not very encouraging because, let us face the fact, I had never done it before and had to learn on the job. Indeed, my early efforts looked as though a family of mice had munched their way through the felt-like undergrowth of follicles.

But I was a quick study and in no time my business was running at a profit. Lesson One in the PoW book of rules has to be: 'Whichever service you provide, get paid for it in provisions.' Translated into the hair cutting business, this comes to half a piece of bread or half a kasha per haircut. Sometimes, I admit, there was a slight argument about the fee, but the business worked sufficiently well for my stomach to stop rumbling. My PoW business philosophy helped me survive during the lean times, and was put to good use whenever one had a need to boost the daily intake of calories.

Regardless of whether it was filling, or even sufficient to remove the feeling of hunger, all camps where I found myself displayed a large board by the dining hall, listing the calories in what we were going to eat. For example: 150g peas (75 cal), 500g cabbage (675 cal), 50g fish (125 cal), 350g kasha (800 cal) = total 1675 calories. The board would also show the regulation allowance of 1500 calories, so we could see that the camp was feeding us 175 calories more than required.

Our camp administrators pointed out that, thanks to Stalin and the Communist Party, if one took into account the 500g of bread we had each day (600 cal), we, the ungrateful, received over 2,000 calories each day. The message was "Be grateful and work for your upkeep. Long live the Party of the Motherland!"

Oh my darling mother, if you saw your carefully nurtured son now greedy and slobbering, gulping down his fish eye soup, what would you think? What became of all your careful upbringing?

But to return to day four. Something had changed. The rain had stopped and the guards took this as a sign that we must be moving on. With sadness and great foreboding, we bade farewell to the abandoned luxuries of yesteryear.

We skirted the next village and found ourselves on the way to Bruno (Brünn). By evening another estate was reached and commandeered so once more we had a roof over our heads. My group was quartered in rooms on the top floor, so once again we had a good view to console us. Looking down from the window as evening drew on, I noticed that Russian soldiers and PoWs were engaging in lively bartering. Whatever valuables the German troops possessed, they were trading for food. This seemed to me an excellent idea. There had been no soup kitchen today, and one could not even guess when there might be one, so I decided to have a go myself.

Rummaging through my possessions, I came across a stopwatch and, recalling the Russians' liking for watches, I took it downstairs. I had found out along the way, that somewhere in Tabor our sentries had liberated a large quantity of ketchup and toasted bread, which obviously needed to be spread around. Bread and ketchup would keep me going for a while, if I could pull off a deal.

One of the Soviet soldiers seemed to be particularly friendly, so, with the help of a comrade who had a smattering of Russian, I approached him. By a combination of basic Russian, basic German and a great deal of gesticulation and body language, he eventually came to understand that I was prepared to trade for a sack of biscuits and some bottles of ketchup a rather special watch. He grinned, pulled up one sleeve of his tunic and displayed an armful of wristwatches.

However, when I showed him what I had to offer, his eyes almost popped out of their sockets. I gave him an old-fashioned street-market pitch and, by pressing various buttons, made the hands move separately and together, and pointed out that this particular invention was far superior to anything he had seen before in the world of watches.

I explained to him how simple it was to operate this magnificent stopwatch. Not withstanding our language problems, I made him understand that all he had to do was look at one of the watches strapped to his arm, remember that time and then press the start button of the stopwatch. Much later, when he wanted to know the exact time, all he had to do was to remember the time when he started the stopwatch, press the stop button, add the elapsed time showing on the stopwatch and – hey presto – he would have the precise time.

Much to my surprise, he swallowed the entire presentation, and I received a bag of bread and a few bottles of ketchup. I have often wondered whether he was ever able to tell the correct time. Fortunately I never saw him again, though maybe this feat of calculation may have helped him gain promotion.

Although we were left in peace on the following day, I had a premonition that something was going to happen to us quite soon. It is a well-known fact that to control any group of people, let alone several thousand PoWs, the trick is to keep them continually off-balance. The strange effect of being subjected to this treatment is that one becomes ultra-sensitive, almost psychic. The seers of ancient Greece may have read entrails, but we tried to read the situation from the little that we could see.

We were intrigued that beyond our compound, in a fenced-off area rather like a horse corral, a fair-sized tent was erected. Then we saw that sentries had been posted all around the enclosure.

The following morning we discovered that large numbers of women had been keeping company with us German troops during the previous days' marches. It seemed that many of them had been accompanying their husbands, but the time had come for them to be separated. We also learned that other women were civilians pressed into our one thousand strong group, simply to keep up the numbers when German soldiers managed to escape.

During the morning these poor women were led across the yard to the new enclosure. Their cries were heartbreaking, and their faces streamed with tears. It was one of the most demoralising scenes we fighting men had to witness. The callousness of the separation was too gut-wrenching for us to put into words. We could only stand and watch and listen.

Not all the women were even German, but that did not matter. So many females counted, it seemed, were females regardless of their nationality. Nothing else mattered.

I subsequently found that this practice was quite common. There was almost a fetish of maintaining the integrity of tally rolls whether the subjects were male or female. On one occasion I even came across a group of French soldiers being treated like PoWs.

It seems they had been held originally in a German PoW camp but when they were liberated by Soviet troops they were put on a train and shipped to the USSR. They may have been on their way home, but they remained under guard as if they were enemies. It took the Russians nearly two months to realise that not only were the French uniforms different from ours, but that the French language was not exactly the same as German!

But back to the girls. Halfway through the morning, a couple of lorries arrived, packed with more women who were all herded into the fenced-off area beyond our own compound. The tent was apparently used as an interrogation centre. No one seemed to stay there very long before emerging on the other side with a piece of paper in their hands. We never did find out what was the purpose of the paper, but the following morning we found that all the womenfolk had gone.

The general consensus was that they had been shipped to special camps in order to work in the coal mines or on collective farms. How many survived I have absolutely no idea, though a few found their way, two years later, to one of the coal pit camps where I was being employed.

It turned out that it was once again our turn to get back on the road. We plodded along for the whole day, talking little, but ceaselessly turning thoughts over in our heads. Step after step, following the man in front. Don't think about the destination, but only about when there may be something to eat or drink or a place to rest.

At the end of the day we came upon a very large complex built around and over a hill. Judging by the layout, it had been designed as an army barracks. Across the valley lay the ruins of an airfield covered with masses of destroyed fighters, bombers and transport planes, every one of which bore German insignia. One came to the conclusion that, rather than leave good equipment to the Russians, the German Air Force had blown up the lot. The camp was huge. It was the collecting point for all German PoWs and at times there must have been more than ten thousand waiting around to find out what the Fates had in store for them.

Each block of one thousand men was placed as an entire group in a separate compound. From our own quarters, on the summit of the hill, we could overlook the complete site. Some way away were herds of horses running in fenced paddocks. Others were being driven towards the camp, headed, it seemed, for a monstrously large kitchen, presumably erected to feed the massed German prisoners. Thanks to the Czech horse population our food supply was secure.

We stayed in that camp for a couple of weeks. There was nothing for us to do, so we mostly walked about our compound in small groups and talked about the past, and our plans for the distant future.

Our present situation we more or less accepted, for nothing we could think of would influence how that turned out.

Each day we marched downhill and collected our portion of horse meat in brodo, the now famous kasha and a piece of bread. My hair cutting business flourished, and I ate well enough of the pretty disgusting food to actually put on a bit of weight.

Day by day, blocks of one thousand men were called up on parade and eventually our turn came. With our meagre belongings, we were lined up by the medical centre. Once inside, we had to strip so that army doctors, male and female, could check and record our bodily appearance, making special note of any wound scars and visible ailments. We were also weighed.

For reasons not made known to us, we were each marked on the upper left arm with one, two, three or four strokes.

Wanting to stay together, our little group of officers watched tensely to see how many marks our comrades were awarded. We were at a loss to follow the logic of the marking, though once we were formed up outside, the one to three-strokers were stood on one side, the four-strokers on the other.

The four-strokers were in the minority. Their numbers had to be made up so there would still be one thousand men in the block, and replacements were taken from those who emerged next from the medical building. One thousand strong we began, and one thousand we would continue to be.

Right face, by the left, quick march and off we went to a waiting train.

As time went by, someone managed to solve the mystery of the body marking. It denoted degrees of usefulness. A single stroke meant the man was in first class condition; two strokes indicated that he was not totally fit, but was acceptable; three strokes that he was not up to much, but still usable. Those with four strokes were so sick or malnourished that they could not be put to work. The four-strokers boarded a different train and were sent home. Pity we did not know earlier. One could have appropriated one of the marking pens quite easily and added strokes to make up four!

Our train was put together from a large number of Russian cattle trucks (twice the size of normal West European ones). Fifty prisoners were put into each truck and, to accommodate the one thousand men in our block, the train was twenty trucks long. The sliding doors were slammed home, the key bolt dropped into its eyepiece, and we settled down on the floor as best as we could. We knew for certain that we would not be 'Scoro damoy' for light years.

The train started to roll, and the monotonous ratata-ratata of the wheels hitting the joints of the rails soon made us sleepy. We settled down to accept our fate. I still had my compass and ascertained that we were heading first to the east and then south-east so, thanks to my geography teacher at school, I had a reasonable idea of where we were going.

South-east from Czechoslovakia lay Hungary, so when daylight came, I watched through the small window high up in the side of the truck for any Hungarian sounding names when we passed through a station. My assessment had been right. We passed right across Hungary and eventually entered Romania. Every six hours or so, the train stopped and the doors were opened. A sentry stood guard so nobody could escape.

While the train rolled unsteadily along, we had to attend to our ablutions by standing or sitting over a small square opening next to the door. Some of us had a fair bout of diarrhoea, while we were all pretty weak on our legs and not too steady when crouching over the 'pot'. Not surprisingly, our aim was, at times, not very accurate.

The poor fellow who had to sleep next to the loo-hole had therefore to get up each time it was used, and afterwards had to clean his sleeping space. By general consent it was agreed that no one person was to suffer by lying in that least desirable of spaces, so we drew up a rota of changing places. When my turn came, I found it preferable to stand throughout the whole period. The atmosphere was abominable, though we were able to open the four windows up near the roof to get a draught which swept away the worst of the stench.

Early in the morning of the fourth day of our trans-continental tour, the train slowed down. The prolonged lurching of the wagon indicated that we were rolling through a large marshalling yard. Every time we ran over a set of points, which jerked the truck into a new direction, we unwilling passengers were flung against each other.

Looking out of the window I saw by the station sign that we had arrived in 'Brasov' (Kronstadt), the capital of Siebenbürgen. It lay at the heart of a region which was mostly populated by Germans whose ancestors had emigrated from Saxony in the Middle Ages. Now Romanian by nationality, they had nevertheless maintained their original national characteristics so it was no surprise to us that, when the train came eventually to a halt, the doors were not opened, and we were not allowed any exercise. Sadly, we did not receive any food either.

However, and now comes a most, if not the most, extraordinary story of my venture into the unknown. The voice of a girl was heard whispering through the floorboards, in German, saying, "Drop me a note with your names and any message for your relatives. I have an aunt in America to whom I will write and pass the message on."
Considering that there were sentries all round, and that one must surely be standing in front of our car as well, this brave girl, whoever she was, gambled with her life in trying to make contact with us.

I wrote a note as she suggested, scribbling down my name and the words:
"Ich bitte Sie höflichst an die obige Addresse zu schreiben, daß es mir gut geht. Man soll ohne Sorge sein. Hoffe vom Lager aus schreiben zu können."
"I am asking you to kindly write to the above address that I am well. Nobody should worry. Hope to be able to write from the camp."
At the end of the note I wrote my signature.

Herrn Carl Jost
Berlin- Steglitz
Albrechtstrasse: 78 II

Ich bitte Sie höflichst an obige Adresse zu schreiben, dass es mir gut geht. Man soll ohne Sorge sein. Hoffe vom Lager aus schreiben zu können.

Hans Joachim Jost

The Note

When I came home after almost five years, on the first page of a folder containing all the correspondence between my parents and myself, from the first day of the war on to the last postcard from Russia, was a letter from a Mrs Mary Hugel, 348 Harrison Street, Gary, Ind., USA. It was dated August 1946, censored by the US Civil Censorship, and in it she not only informed my parents of the message which she had received from her niece, but she also enclosed that very note which I had written in Kronstadt in May 1945. Whilst I was travelling east, the note had travelled halfway around the globe and back. It reached its intended recipient just one year after my parents had received their first sign that I was alive, on Christmas Eve 1945. I treasure that letter and its contents in gratitude to the girl who risked her own freedom to help those whom she never met and never knew.

32

Mary Hugel
348 Harrison Str.
Gary Ind.
U.S.A.

gary Ind. 3 august 1946

Herr Fost!

Herrn.

Carl Fost
Berlin - Steglitz
albrecht strasse N 78 II
Germany

GARY, IN
AUG 5
12 - M
1946

UNITED STATES POSTAGE

U.S. CIVIL CENSORSHIP
GERMANY

OPENED BY

The Letter

That night we remained in the siding and watched through the little windows our Red Army soldiers' camp-fires and listened to their songs. Some of the voices were outstanding, from the highest soprano to the deepest baritone. Their yearning stretched out to us. This night brought home to me the deep melancholy of the Russian soul, their love for life when they danced to the tune of the balalaika, and the nostalgia of the Russian people. The fires and the songs died down, but we could not sleep. We just rested, thinking of home and hoping that the messages we had entrusted to that unknown girl would, by some magic, reach there.

The following morning, we were shunted to and fro and got underway again. Not very far, as it turned out. Just down to Focsani, a large town north of Bucharest. Our train stopped and we disembarked at long last.

Lined up for the now customary frisking, we advanced slowly, settled on the ground and waited until everyone had been searched and the Russians were satisfied that we were not in possession of any heavy artillery or the odd hand-grenade. After a short walk across the field, we entered a large – a very large – camp in which at any one time some ten thousand prisoners were collected and sorted for onward transportation. The weather was holding and we could walk about at our leisure.

A jazz band had been formed from musicians who, as civilians, had been snatched from Breslau, in Silesia, and who had to play for the amusement of the crowd to take their mind off their plight. How simple minded the Soviets were, thinking that it only took a bit of dance music to make us happy.

With a steady intake of prisoners, the camp began to burst at its seams, despite the departure of transports almost daily. The kitchen block was not large enough to cope with all those hungry mouths and had to be enlarged. Plans were drawn up and preparations made to commence building. What with, we wondered. Though there was sand and cement for the mortar, we could see no bricks.

One night a train full of bricks arrived and a working party was detailed to unload it. This they did, throwing the bricks out of the wagons on to the open field.

How would the great pile of bricks be transported to where construction could take place? We were in for a display of ingenuity of which only the simple working minds of our Russian minders were capable.

Well organised, sophisticated Western armies would have lined up a column of lorries, each manned by a gang, driven to the brick dump, loaded the trucks by stacking the bricks in neat rows and then carted the whole lot to the kitchen site where they would have been unloaded and re-stacked nicely. The exercise would have taken all day, consumed an awful lot of petrol and necessitated afterwards the cleaning and scrubbing of the vehicles to army regulation standards.

Not so with our friends. You need a few thousand bricks at the kitchen and you need them there quickly? 'Ladna' – good, you have got it. Wakey, wakey! All German prisoners rise and line up at the gate. You want your morning meal, then you can earn it. Out you go to the brick mountain, you lot, take two bricks each under your arms and walk back to the camp kitchen. Stockpile the lot where you are told and then go and get your rations. Inside two hours twenty thousand bricks were transferred from A to B.

The days dragged by, and so far as we could tell, nothing was happening. Come rain or sunshine, we were not allowed to stay inside the huts, although we never found out why.

To kill the time, discussion groups were formed and lectures given on a wide variety of subjects. Someone organised language lessons, particularly Russian and, oddly enough, French. Rumours circulated like wildfire, buzzing from one end of the camp to the other.
"Have you heard, there is going to be a large transport home because they can't cope with so many prisoners."
"No, no, we are going to be sent to Siberia to work as lumberjacks and in the coal mines."
"The Red Cross is going to visit us in the next few days and will be distributing parcels," and so on.

There was some truth in all of them. The Red Cross never came, but we received parcels four years later. Some of the prisoners were sent to Siberia and others, like us, ended up in the forests and the coal mines, in that order.

We stopped counting the days and resigned ourselves to our fate, waiting for whatever was to come. And come it did, suddenly. In the middle of one night we were herded to a waiting train, all one thousand of our block of PoWs, shoved into the wagons and off we went.

The two days that the journey took were the worst we ever had or would experience. Every so often, the train stopped, we were chased out of our carriages and frisked to the bone. All medals and orders, all regimental badges or insignias, and all shoulder straps were ripped off. We were beaten and kicked.

What on earth had happened? The guards had changed and we saw that none of them wore any medals or were showing any signs that they had ever been at the Front. That was the answer, without a doubt. On all sides in a war, those who have seen action respect their opponents. Once the war was over, it was bad luck that you lost but there were no hard feelings. But we were now in the hands of youngsters, some with the badge of the 'Young Pioneers', an organisation somewhat similar to the Hitler Youth. They could, and did, vent their anger on those who could no longer defend themselves. These were two exceedingly long days and nights.

The end of this part of our journey proved to be at Constanta, the main Romanian port. We were turned out of the train and kicked into some sort of formation to march through town. All along the route, Romanians tried to cheer us up, offering food and even intimating that they would help anyone who wanted to escape. But the guards had been doubled, or even tripled, to prevent any such attempts and made sure that they delivered their charges to the last man. It was a mortifying, slow march. The last drop of spirit had effectively been beaten out of what once had been one of the most feared and respected army units, Schörner's 5th Army Corps.

We assembled at the quayside next to a freighter of no more than five thousand tons. Over the gangway we went, and into the hold. After all, she was a freighter and we were nothing more than freight. But when you squeeze a thousand men into a hold which was more suited to sand and gravel, timber and tar barrels, you quickly find out that men do not stack like freight.

There was very little room for lying down and one was forced to stand upright like so many candles in a box. If one were really lucky, one could sit on the floor. My sea-legs were never good and I feared the coming sea journey, not that I had much in my stomach to offer up to Neptune. However, if it came to that, I wanted to keep the little I had where it was.

With the ship still moored, it was baking hot in the hold. The air was stale and all we could see was a bit of blue sky through the hatch and the sentries, bayonets fixed, who were surrounding this unlikely escape route like beanstalks circling a vegetable bed.

In the afternoon the ropes were cast off and we steamed out into the Black Sea. Where to? After much questioning we were told that our destination would be Odessa, some two hundred miles away. The journey took two days. That old rust bucket could not have done more than eight knots. She was powered by a coal-fired steam engine, which, judged by the noise and the vibration it made, must have been designed by James Watt and discarded by him as a failure. On the second day of our pleasure trip we were allowed on deck, presumably because we had left Romanian territorial waters and were under the watchful eyes of the Soviet Navy, not that we saw any warships. It was a great relief to be able to breathe fresh sea air, and to gaze miles and miles across the blue sea. Odessa came into sight, the ship stopped and dropped anchor in the bay. After nightfall we docked. Officers were separated from the rest, and disembarked first. We stepped ashore and set foot once more on Soviet soil, at a spot remarkably close to where I had been four years earlier. We had come full circle.

OFFICERS ARE NO GENTLEMEN

By this time, naturally enough, we were all feeling pretty fed up. It is one thing to be captured in battle, but quite another to be taken prisoner after the cease-fire. Our being shipped off to Russia seemed downright unfair! It was also immensely disquieting.

The future looked bleak and all that we could do was live each day as it came along and hope for the best. I firmly believed that everything would come right eventually and that somehow, some time, I would get back home. For the moment, though, the name of the game was survival.

Our first night in Odessa was mild. We straggled through sparsely lit, deserted streets with our only guard an unarmed corporal. This was itself somewhat alarming, for presumably nobody thought there was much risk we would run away. In actual fact the Romanian border was so close that some of us could indeed have made an attempt to escape.

Just what would happen if, having run off, we were later to be recaptured? It was every PoW's right under the Geneva Convention to make every effort to escape, but no doubt recapture would bring punishment. Where did the Soviet Union stand on the issue? From wartime experience, unfortunately, we knew that neither the Germans, the British nor the Americans recognised that 'enshrined' right to escape.

These thoughts certainly occupied my mind as we meandered along, until we came to a district with tall, elegant houses built at some time in the eighteenth century and stopped outside a huge wooden gate. A narrow doorway let into the wall beside the gate opened into a large enclosed courtyard. The setting was so unexpected after our travels and, despite our near despair, struck us all as being quite romantic. There was a solitary cast-iron lamppost throwing long shadows across the stonework.

Another soldier came out to take a set of papers from our guide and to arrange a hasty roll-call to make sure there were no stragglers. Only when that was completed were we directed to a building running down one side of the courtyard. Off to these quarters went our small party consisting of Wurzelzwerg and twenty-six officers. In true army fashion we immediately set about making ourselves comfortable.

I woke early next morning and looked out at the houses opposite, which were indeed in a style of the late eighteenth century, rising four storeys with majestic, full-paned windows about 1.8 m (6ft) tall. All had louvred shutters opening outwards and held in place against the walls by large cast-iron toggles. Ground floor windows were fitted with elegant wrought iron guards, curving out into the yard like small balconies and sweeping back to where S-shaped brackets attached them firmly to the wall.

The houses had once been painted a warm yellow with white window frames and trellises, but all was now faded and soiled. The last time a painter had been employed there was quite obviously long before the War.

The courtyard itself was of fairly modest size and paved in cobblestones. Two widely-spaced rows of plane trees embraced long wooden tables and benches, looking for all the world like a set from some light opera. The scene was quite entrancing and hinted that good wine and tasty food would soon be laid out for our pleasure. Such dreams!

Near the exit the courtyard funnelled into a passageway, and beyond was the gate though which we had entered. A guard now stood there looking curiously and watchfully at the small group of prisoners loitering away their time.

At eight o'clock or thereabouts, we were called for a roll-call and lined up in front of the trees. We were counted, found to be all present and correct and ordered to wait for a few minutes. Then, from the centre door of the main building appeared the majestic figure of a Russian major in the dress uniform of the political forces, complete with shiny medals. Chief among these emblems was the golden star of 'Hero of the Soviet Union'. He made it very clear that he was the Camp Commandant.

With mixed feelings we noted that he had a Jewish cast of face; mixed, because, although as former front line troops we had been far removed from any involvement in Hitler's 'Final Solution', one could not help wondering how hard a line he proposed taking with us.

Grim-faced, he slowly walked down our line, looking deeply into everyone's eyes, then stood back a few paces. We expected antagonism and were quite unprepared for the mournful address that was to come. In impeccable and fluent German, he declared, "I was promised that I would be in charge of German combat officers. Instead, what do I see? A bunch of ragged-looking figures who might just as well be a bunch of tramps, judging by the sorry state of your clothing."

This was hardly surprising, considering how we had been treated during our journey, the cattle-car transportation to Constanta and the appalling conditions we had been obliged to endure on the boat. When our Wurzelzwerg stood to attention and explained all this, the camp commandant cross-examined him, seeking out the most minute details. He wrote in his notebook the serial number of our cattle truck, as well as descriptions of the Russian soldiers who had stolen our gear.

To our great surprise he announced finally, "This crime shall not go unpunished. One does not treat a former enemy like dirt."
Pointing to his medals and the golden star, he continued, "I was in the firing line myself. I fought brave opponents; I want them treated properly."
With those astonishing words he dismissed us until further notice.

The next couple of days seemed like a peaceful monastic retreat. Occasionally, traffic noise would penetrate our quarters as a reminder of the world outside, but we happily filled in the time playing chess or talking about the good old days before the War, and about our homes and relatives. We had no photos to share, of course, because along with all our other possessions these were presumably the proud spoils of the heroic Komsomolsk juvenile soldiers.

With a crash and a rumble, the gate opened on the third day to allow a huge military lorry to drive into our courtyard. We just had time to recognise that it was manned by some of our earlier tormentors when the Camp Commandant appeared on the scene, and made the Soviet soldiers spread the lorry's entire contents on the ground before forming up next to the vehicle.

We were summoned into the yard. Did we recognise any of the Red Army soldiers? If so, we were to point them out to him. With considerable pleasure we obliged. Next we were told to look for any personal possessions, medals and insignia of rank and, when we found what had belonged to us, we watched in utter disbelief as the Major arrested all those who had misbehaved so grievously towards us. No doubt they would shortly have the pleasure of pacing a gulag in Siberia.

"Take your stuff," the Major ordered, "go to your quarters, clean yourselves, put on your decorations and shoulder straps and assemble here again in one hour sharp."

With a smart about-turn, he went off one way and we went the other. Exactly one hour later we reassembled in ranks, with Wurzelzwerg up front. The Major stepped from his quarters; our colonel called us to attention and reported to him the assembled officers.

Thanking him with a military salute, the Major stepped back and addressed us again.

"Now I see German officers I am satisfied." He continued, "Gentlemen, you have been unlucky twice in your life: firstly you lost the War; secondly, you fell into the hands of the Soviet Union. Not that this is too bad. But soon you will be very far away from home, much further away than if you had been able to join our Western Allies. All the same, I bid you welcome to the Soviet Union. Dismissed."

What an extraordinary thing to happen. Not just the address by the NKWD Major, but the unbelievable way he treated his own soldiers, as well as his help in recovering at least some of our belongings.

I now had back in my pocket the photos of my parents, my driving licence, toiletry gadgets, razor and everything else. If this was a sign of things to come, I thought, being a PoW might not be all that bad. Unfortunately, we were to learn only too quickly that this was the shiny side of a coin that was much more sombre when turned over.

A week later, just as we were finishing our midday meal, we were asked to gather up our things and assemble in the yard, whereupon the Major appeared and announced that we were going to be transferred to another camp, wishing us, "Good luck." Military salutes were duly given and returned and off we marched, leaving the major standing in the middle of the courtyard watching us go. I felt a trifle sorry for this lonely, grand old man in his resplendent uniform. Thank you Major, I thought, for having restored our belief in humanity.

Our new camp, outside the town and close to the shores of the Black Sea, was part of a warehouse complex which had been cordoned off with barbed wire, with watchtowers on all four corners. The small shed to which we were assigned was just large enough to accommodate our group. It was furnished with bunk-beds and, luxury of luxuries, each had its own luxurious straw mattress. How glorious this would be after weeks of sleeping on bare floors.

By the end of the day the other barracks filled up with the balance of our thousand men contingent, so we were all together again.

It was here that I had my introduction to that living torture instrument, teeth on legs, which pestered me whenever I lay on, or even sat on, my bed. Yes, we had a plague of bugs! They were everywhere, and everyone suffered. Thousand upon thousand of them: baby bugs, small bugs, large bugs, giant bugs. Little did I know then, that I was to encounter them in every single camp from now to the end of my Russian tour.

We took our beds apart, removed the boards and shook them. We hit those bugs as they fell off the boards, we squashed them and flamed them. If anyone is interested, the smell of burnt bed-bugs is like squashed bitter almonds... revolting.

The Americans seemed to be aware of this Russian secret weapon for, in addition to sending over tanks and Studebaker lorries as part of their wartime aid to their Red ally, they had consigned a supply of DDT, the latest in pest control. Regrettably little of it was to be found in our camp, and the sample we received was far too small to do much good. So, as the nights were warm and dry, I got into the habit of moving my mattress outside to sleep under the stars.

On a clear night it was always easy to pick out the constellation of Orion, its belt pointing the way home. The star on the right was in the east, the one on the left in the west. Should I ever want to make my own way back, I would have these clear markers to follow.

To some extent, I suppose, we were glad to be in what was obviously no more than a transit camp, as there was always the hope that our lot would improve once we arrived at our final destination. There was a railway siding close to our hut, and we had a good view as transports regularly came down from all over the complex to move out of the area.

One compensation for being in that camp was that we were allowed down to the beach each day for a swim in the Black Sea. How refreshing and relaxing this was. After two weeks, though, we received the order to board a train so we could get to our next camp. Perhaps this would be our last journey for a long time.

Once again we were crammed into cattle trucks. Hour upon hour these rumbled and rolled along, with infrequent stops at small stations. The railway line was mostly single track and our transport was frequently driven into sidings where we waited while normal commercial traffic passed. At times these delays were quite prolonged but, as we were permitted to leave the doors open, we did not mind all that much. After all, it made no difference what time we turned up wherever we were going. Now and again, we could relieve the tedium by disembarking and stretching our legs.

Travelling with open doors was itself an improvement on some of the journeys we had suffered. We could now take an interest in the countryside or, when this lost its edge, we took it in turns simply to sit on the edge with our legs dangling over the side and dream the day away. All in all, it was rather relaxing. One thing we were learning from the experience was the vast size of the country, for it seemed to us that no trip in Russia could be accomplished in a single day.

On the fourth day the train was running along a track that was as straight as a ruler. Whichever door we looked through, the view was the same. As far as the horizon, on each side of the train, were fields of maize and young wheat interspersed with crops of watermelon. The vastness of the Ukrainian landscape was even greater than we remembered from the recent days of war when the German Army had advanced across this land before being forced to retreat. Of course, on our earlier visit the earth had been shattered by shell fire, and the days and nights filled with the sound of automatic guns and rocket launchers, and the droning of aircraft.

How peaceful it all looked now, with not the slightest hint that ten thousands of men and women had lost their lives for this piece of earth, which was now recovering from the mutilation it had had to endure. Small villages came and went as we trundled by, each one looking like a plate from some history book, as though the clock had been turned back one hundred and more years.

They were timber houses, in the main, with small gardens where the Soviet government allowed peasants to grow a few vegetables and keep a cow or a pig as reward for being drafted into the Kolchos, the state controlled co-operatives, in which they slaved day and night to feed the Russian population.

The Ukraine, which had once been Polish territory, would always be the granary of the heartland of Russia. To Georgia and the smaller republics in the south of the empire, it was not so important for they had plenty of food and were self-sufficient. So it was the industrialised part of Russia that really suffered from the inefficiency, disorganisation and corruption of the western region. I would soon gain first-hand experience of that chaos.

The area through which we passed was so depressing that it was almost fitting that, whenever our rolling cage stopped for the night, we could hear melancholic, not to say downright mournful, songs drifting over the fields. Incidentally, the huge doors of our luxurious carriages were shut up tight as soon as darkness fell so we could only judge our surroundings by what we could hear.

During the night the train changed direction to head northwards and the next morning we saw changes in the landscape, too. We avoided any large towns or cities, but as the day wore on we could see that agriculture was steadily replaced by a fair degree of industry.

During one stop we called over to some bystanders to try to find out the name of the nearest big town, and learned that we were nearing Kursk. Memories came flooding back, for this was the scene of the largest and fiercest tank battle of our Eastern campaign two years earlier. Already the scars had healed and there was absolutely no sign of the fighting that had taken place. Ruined villages had been rebuilt, fields restored, and new trees planted where only stumps had remained on the battlefield after the scorched earth retreat. How quickly time heals the wounds; how quickly one forgets the horrors of war.

Looking at the reborn area, it is quite astonishing that I felt no remorse about what had happened. After all, we had been pawns in a great game of power and domination, moved around the board according to passing ideologies designed to serve ridiculous politics. From our aspect, the War had been neither grand nor amusing. It was frightening: it was cold; it was bloody; it was appalling. Warfare in the early Middle Ages had been much more humane, despite all the slaughter associated with it. In those far-off days the leaders on both sides fought it out between them, after which the army of the loser went home. Woyna kaput. Si chass damoy.

Because I 'knew' the region from bitter experience, I knew that if the train maintained its heading we would hit Voronezh, but it did not.

We found ourselves going south once more, then continuing eastwards, so we became convinced that the object was to avoid all built-up areas.

At the end of the day, after the trail led north-east, we arrived at a large siding in a place called Penza. And where, I wondered, was Penza? It was nowhere on the map I carried around in my head, so guesswork was the order of the day. Guess where we were, guess where we were heading for, guess whether we would end up in Siberia, guess what would happen to us at all. Before very long I realised that this would lead me nowhere, except up the path to insanity.

There was nothing any of us could do. We had no alternative but to recognise that our future lay in the hands of Joseph Stalin, back in the Kremlin. One thing was certain, though. The further east we were transported, the less certain we became of an early return home.

On the sixth day after leaving Odessa we pulled out of Penza en route for Saransk. The locomotive was changed and the train proceeded very slowly along a track that led north, into a region covered with birch forests stretching as far as the eye could see. Clearings in the forests held small settlements and scattered timber huts whose front gardens were lovingly tended by the inhabitants.

Eventually the trees receded, and in a large clearing appeared a detention camp complete with watchtowers, high fences and guards. At first sight it seemed practically deserted, but as the train drew closer we could see some drab figures scurrying about. They did not look like PoWs and we concluded that they were probably conscripts.

We did not stop there, though, but slowly drew up the line until another camp became visible and then, and after a few more kilometres, another one. Quite clearly the single railway track we were on served all the camps in this area, and it soon dawned on us that we were in the middle of one of the detention districts one had heard so much about. It took another hour or so for our transport to come to a halt, at a place where one camp was on the left of the line and one on the right. The one on our left seemed much larger and was occupied. We officers were ordered to disembark, along with one hundred other ranks and hastened to the smaller camp on our right. The rest of our mob was led to the larger compound.

We had arrived at Lager (Camp) 58/6, otherwise known as Yavas.

It took no time at all to size up our situation. Wooden barracks lined a large yard on three sides. A further building, set to the rear, seemed to be a workshop, judging by the sound of a circular saw and noises similar to those of wood being chopped. After a short count of our uneasy-looking lot we were told to disperse and take up quarters.

We arranged ourselves into groups. Those who had come to know each other best during the past weeks marched off to see what kind of accommodation had been provided for our benefit. Each barrack building was about twenty metres long and equipped with two rows of bunk benches, on either side of a wide aisle. I immediately jumped on the top platform and took up occupation of a space which I could call my own, although I recognised it would be somewhat cramped, as the hut had to accommodate one hundred and twenty men. No sooner had we sorted ourselves out than we went outside again and started to explore our new abode. Drawn by the woodworking noise, I went to the building at the rear.

There I saw ten PoWs sitting on primitive workbenches, chopping away at wooden blocks with small, extremely sharp axes. Each man had a template and I soon realised that what they were actually doing was producing wooden shoe soles. Elsewhere, men were cutting canvas to size and shape and nailing these to the soles with the efficiency that comes from considerable experience. The shoes they were making were of the very type we would all be wearing before long.

Further back in the compound, and separated by a partition, stood an old diesel generator which was being nursed along by a PoW. It was supposed to produce the electricity required to drive the circular saw on which the raw material was cut to size, as well as power the few electrical bulbs dangling from the ceiling. I quickly discovered that this antiquated old thing was also the sole generator not only for this camp, but for the one across the railway line, as well as the offices and quarters of the Russian administrators and the military.

Our source for all this information, and more, was the group of fellows chopping away at their wooden bricks. Imagine how glad they were to see us, for some of those German PoWs had been in the camp since 1941, having been taken prisoner at the beginning of the war with Russia. Only some fifty of them were in this camp and they had been waiting for us to show up for almost two months, when they were told that they would be having visitors very soon.

Naturally enough, at least at the beginning of our stay here, these old hands were the ones who taught us the art of behaving as prisoners of the Russians. At that time they had charge of such camp services as the bakery, the kitchen and the other, less demanding, chores associated with camp life. But it was not too long before they were swallowed up by the much greater number that had intruded upon their seclusion.

We quickly found out something else – that of all the camps up and down the railway line as far as Gorki, ours was the only one for German PoWs.

The warm and sunny weather was holding, and we were left to our own devices. Apart from two roll counts, one in the morning and one in the late afternoon, nothing happened. We saw few Russians, we were not introduced to the camp commander, and we saw precious little of Wurzelzwerg, who had retreated into a far corner and was pining, perhaps because he had not been given the expected staff quarters as befitted his rank.

The food was adequate, not to say luxurious at times. We got half a pound of soggy bread, kasha and soup at noon and to our surprise one tin of luncheon meat, freshly imported from the USA, between four.

We were also introduced to a staple of the Russian population – machorka. This type of tobacco came in long sticks, was rock hard and had to be finely cut until the result resembled chopped straw as munched by horses. But we had a small problem: there was no paper to roll a cigarette. In actual fact, there was no paper at all for any use whatever. The camp was, in the fullest sense of the word, a timber camp. Notes were written down on wooden boards and shingles and erased by scrubbing with a piece of metal, or the sharp edge of a stone or the like. Paper was very precious and we were urged to save it whenever and wherever we could, much like the citizens of Caesar's Rome!

The main problem of a paperless society was going to the latrine. We were quite unaccustomed to wiping our honourable behinds with birch bark which, I know from experience, is, to say the least, rather uncomfortable. So we had to resort to the age-old custom adopted by Arabs, Tartars and other well educated latrine-goers. We learned to keep clean water close to hand and wash ourselves off each time.

We had to learn many things which had never been covered at my grammar school. What has this to do with machorka? Quite a lot. As there could be no cigarette smoking if there was no paper, quite obviously we would have to get some pipes. Clearly we could not pop out to the local shop to buy one, so my mates and I set to and made ourselves pipes from birch. First we looked around for branches of a suitable diameter and then hollowed it out to form a bowl and stem. To prevent the machorka dust from entering the mouthpiece we fitted a fly button from Prussian uniform trousers as a filter.

The pipe I made in that camp I still have today, button and all, reminding me of Timberland. How did the machorka taste? It is hard to describe, but essentially it was an amalgam of sweet-smelling highland grass and Chinese tea. When rolled in a piece of newspaper taken, say, from *Pravda* or the *Red Army News*, it has an overpowering flavour said to be similar to that of opium, not that I have ever tasted opium! Personally I feel it must be very much like the stuff which produces Soviet fog. Since watching cadres of krassnyi rabotschiks (red workers) smoking machorka and experiencing at firsthand the smoke they produced, I now knew where the fog came from. In terms of today's scientific discoveries, the distribution and consumption of machorka must have contributed greatly to the 'greenhouse effect' of global warming.

A major problem we had to surmount was how to cut bread, carve our pipes, and perform any other task for which a knife was necessary when all our knives had been taken away, without our getting suitable replacements.

This seemed to us at the time as being typical Russian thinking. On one hand they gave us lethal weapons in the shape of razor-sharp tomahawks to make wooden-soled shoes, but on the other made sure that we had no knives. It took us a long time to convince the camp's political commissar that the days when Germans stabbed Russian citizens were now gone. After that, though still unofficially, we were allowed to make small cutting tools which were mostly more lethal than big machetes. Just as I still have my cherished pipe, so do I also have the knife which I made from the blade of a hacksaw. Without having ever been sharpened, it can be offered to one's chin as a razor to scrape off the stubble without cutting through the skin.

One of our camp comrades, called Hege, had been an explorer, having grown up in Bolivia and stayed on to explore South America, paying particular attention to the Andes. He was sturdily built and had silver-grey hair, cut short, atop an almost square head. He continually wore a soft, relaxed and kind expression. Before long he began giving lectures on his numerous exploits.

"Endurance and patience, combined with a rigid determination to succeed, good physical and mental health, an innate ability to be inventive and, if called for, the ability to talk one's way out of any difficult situation in order to survive, are the pre-requisites of an explorer," he explained. "Of course," he continued, "one must have the powers of observation and be able to keep a meticulous written account of the venture, the animal and plant world and geographical conditions. Most important of all, though, one has to return to civilisation so as to publish a book and give lectures in order to rake in money to squander on other silly and exciting explorations."

In his fascinating lectures, Hege radiated the enthusiasm and fire of a man totally dedicated to searching the unknown parts of the world, unravelling mysteries and bringing home the findings. We learnt so much from this man who really should never have been there, for the Russians had picked him up off the street one day when they were rounding up people. He was a civilian. The closest he had ever been to the army was watching a parade.

We had been relieved of our wristwatches, so Hege taught us to read the time by taking account of the sunshine, and eventually we could do this with an accuracy of five to ten minutes, using the very simplest of tools. For the benefit of anyone who may find themselves in a predicament similar to my own, here is Hege's method:

Pick a blade of grass or find a very thin straw and cut it to the length of the distance between the web of the little finger of the left hand and where the nail protrudes from its bed.

Stand the blade vertically on top of the web of the little finger of the left hand and place the other hand, knuckles upwards, and thumb to thumb together. Make both hands horizontal, as nearly as possible. Now turn into the sun until the blade casts a shadow across the hands and in line with the knuckles. Count from left to right each finger, beginning with the ring finger of the left hand, up to the little finger of the right hand and then back to the one where the shadow ends. If the shadow ends in the middle of the finger it is the full hour; between the fingers the half hour. If the shadow ends less to the left or to the right it is the quarter hour, and so on in lesser divisions. Using this method before noon one can determine the time to within 10 minutes.

After noon it's slightly different (one can always tell whether it is morning or afternoon). The blade of grass is placed on the web between the ring finger and the middle finger. Counting starts with the middle finger and the little finger of the left hand is counted twice.

Simple if you know how! Hege's lesson came in handy from then on throughout my stay on Russian soil, every time I needed to know the time. Indeed I still use it if I have left my watch behind.

Our first week started off pleasantly enough. Indeed, the low point seemed to be when the Russian quartermaster ran out of American luncheon meat and we had to return to our basic diet of cabbage soup and kasha. But then things most decidedly took a turn for the worse and we were made to realise that, truly, we were PoWs.

One morning after roll-call we were led across the railway tracks into the larger camp and into the communal bath-house block. We would have to use that from now on. To get a true feel for it we were ordered to discard our uniforms and hand in all military insignia, medals and so on. We looked a pretty sorry sight standing around shivering while we waited for our shower, but then came the further indignity of having all our head, underarm and pubic hair cut off. I shall never forget that at that moment I thought we looked just like convicts, though to be fair it was hard to tell us Germans from the Russian soldiers who also had shaven heads. Presumably their other parts were likewise free of body hair as well. The treatment, we were told, was purely hygienic, to prevent the spread of lice.

After showering we received second-hand Russian uniforms and pairs of those same cloth-covered clogs we had earlier seen being made. So our captors could tell friend from foe, our shirts and jackets were marked with the Cyrillic letters for WP (for Woyna Pleni, or war prisoner).

At this point in my story it is worth recalling the old expression that 'officers are gentlemen'. Under international law it had long been held that, because they were gentlemen, officers could not be made to work when taken prisoner. Now that I, like several thousand others, lacked any badges of rank and had to wear the common rankless uniform, I idly wondered at the time what had become of this part of the Geneva Convention.

The fact of the matter is, that just as the German authorities refused to apply it to Russian PoWs of the rank of captain and below, so the Russians in my day held that anyone of the rank of captain or below should be treated like the troops at large. So it was that I, who had proudly risen to be a captain, found myself very definitely back in the ranks. Strangely, it was almost comforting, in the circumstances, not to stand out too obviously, for I saw this as another important element in my determination to survive.

So it was as an amorphous group of faceless men that we lurched back to our own side of the tracks, to what we now knew to be called Stalag X, and waited to see what other surprises lay in store. The following morning we were issued with empty tin cans and marched off into the woods to gather blueberries, wild strawberries and any other edible berry we could find. We were told our 'norm' was one full tin each. The word 'norm' entered our vocabulary that day and was to haunt us thereafter.

'Norm' meant 'total fulfilment' of any given task, and as the norm was set up ahead of time it also let one know how much one had to do. So when we were collecting berries the norm would be set as one tin or two tins to be filled, or for shoemaking the number of pairs to be made in a day, or for mining the number of tons to be moved... and so on. One hundred percent fulfilment of the norm meant that we would qualify for the full amount of pay or food. If less than one hundred percent of the norm was achieved, there would be a proportionate cutback in one's pay or food. If we exceeded the norm, we did not automatically get extra food, though in due course we found that when payment was fixed for a given job, there would be more cash forthcoming if we exceeded our target. More about that later.

Anyway, on this first work day we went off into the woods where we ate as many berries as we wanted, provided we satisfied the norm. Our guard was an old, gullible and rather naive soldier armed with a German 98k rifle. Through our interpreter we chatted with him and, during a rest period when we sat around as though we were on a picnic, he became very relaxed. He soon seemed convinced that the Germans were not as bad a lot as he had been led to believe. He actually found us quite amicable chaps, really.

He opened his tunic and showed us a huge bundle of rouble notes. This represented his entire fortune, saved a little at a time right through his service in the War. He was soon to be discharged from the army and was looking forward to going back to his home village. What would he do with all that money?

A smile spread right across his face.

"I am going to build myself a nice house, with two bedrooms, a sitting room, a kitchen and an indoor toilet... and central heating."

And what would it look like when it was finished?

"It will be exactly as I saw it in Vienna!"

Oh poor Mushik, I thought, wait until you get home and see how the political commissar will destroy your dreams in no time. Vienna will seem even further away than it was before the War.

With our tins full, we trotted back and handed them in to the hospital, where the fruit was distributed among the sick, after the Russian orderlies had creamed off a share for themselves. The following few days saw me again picking berries and enjoying the comparative freedom.

Shortly after this, I wound up as a patient of the health farm, having developed an atrocious bout of piles. Not on the skin alone, but internally as well. The pain was excruciating. I could neither walk nor stand and spent most of the time crouching on my hands and knees in bed during the day and the night. Now it became my turn to receive juicy wild berries and, wonder of wonders, white bread and semolina pudding instead of the sour and wet mush that passed for bread and kasha in the main body of the camp.

Imagine this: there was absolutely no treatment. Only occasional relief came from sitting in a bowl of cold water. With no medication being available to cure them, I carried these piles with me for the rest of my years as a PoW and eventually aroused the keen interest of the surgeon who took me in hand after my return home and who, to my eternal gratitude, was able to rid me of both the pain and the piles. What a subject to write about, yet as it coloured my every activity during captivity it cannot be glossed over lightly.

As the days went by, with not much to occupy us mentally or physically, I began to understand why the men housed on the other side of the railway line were so much happier than we. Despite the fact that they, too, were prisoners they had the satisfaction of being able to work and produce something of value. So they only produced clogs, but at the end of each day they could see that by using their hands they had something tangible to their credit.

It became clear to me during this period that any kind of activity would keep the little grey cells between the ears moving, so one would be spared cabin fever and the mindless boredom that actually leads to death. I reflected on these philosophical wonderings some ten months later, though, when we were regularly toiling quite literally as slaves.

One morning in August we were called together and handed 'Red Cross and Crescent' postcards, together with lilac coloured ink and nibs (without a nib holder).

"Write home," said the interpreter, "but do not give any details about your actual whereabouts, nor what you are doing."

We could not very well let on about our location because we had not the remotest idea where we were. As to the work on which we were engaged, we could see that the Russians regarded the clogs being made across the tracks as part of some secret weapon yet to be revealed to the United Nations.

Maybe this was not so far off the mark, in actual fact, for one day a certain Mr Krushchev was to take off his shoe to hammer home a point at the UN General Assembly. I wonder if he had been wearing one of our clogs, or some soft-leather copy!

"You may say only that you are still alive and well, are being properly treated, have enough to eat and are looking forward in general to coming home 'scoro budit'," we were advised. Well, I wrote my card hoping it would reach my parents, but doubtful that it would, because I had received a report towards the end of hostilities that my parents' house had been bombed and that they had vanished. Sadly, none of my letters home had been answered.

"Don't worry," we were told. "Your cards will be posted home." To a man we were distinctly sceptical and looked on the whole exercise as a propaganda ploy. Remarkably, though, they were sent and my own card was delivered on Christmas Eve that year.

My parents immediately wrote a long letter in reply, and this reached me without being censored on my birthday the following year. All the stories about bombing and their disappearance, I realised, were not true. Ties with home being re-established; from that day onwards postcards and letters were exchanged quite regularly, though at times with lengthy delays. My father numbered his letters, and as a result I was able to establish that not one failed to arrive.

In later years I was often asked how we had fared and I have had to admit that in time I came to realise we were treated no worse and no better than the Russians treated their own people. Indeed, I feel that at times we were rather better off.

While in transit we had come under Red Army administration. For the rest we were looked after by the KGB, who felt that they need look no further than our own ranks to find the toughs to look after us on their behalf.

The KGB regarded the Austrians among us as the oppressed tribe of the German-speaking population, and often selected them to oversee the working groups. I have to say that these overseers carried out their duties most rigorously, like their compatriots who had volunteered to run the concentration camps, or who had taken major roles in persecuting Jews and members of other 'undesirable races'. (Of course, the world should know that these tormentors were never Nazis; it was mere coincidence that Hitler, Eichmann, and so many of the others were of Austrian ancestry.)

The incredible consequence of this recognition of Austria as an aggrieved party was that the Austrian PoWs were the first to be repatriated. Well, maybe this was only fair, for had they not also been the first outside Germany itself to raise their right arms and shout 'Heil Hitler' and to hail the Führer as their native son for liberating them from the socialists? They rallied in their thousands to the colours of the reunited Greater Germany and flocked to the Waffen SS under General Dietrich.

I have always felt it extraordinary that former comrades-in-arms should glory so in lording it over us German PoWs. Worst of all were those who traditionally had formed the 'backbone of the army' – the lance-corporals and corporals, but then Hitler himself had once been a corporal.

Being in close confinement with people one has known as compatriots and fellows lets one discover things about them that previously remained below the surface. My father used to say, "If you want to get to know your own people, look at them from across the border." I can see that this was very sage advice.

As the month of July ended and August burst upon us, we were assembled with our belongings, led to the main gate, counted yet again and told to proceed to the camp on the opposite side. Before we could enter, we were obliged to stop so that we could be counted again. Counting must be a Russian obsession, I thought. Was it remotely conceivable that anyone could have escaped during the fifty metres' march over to the main camp? But wait, this time we were divided into groups of two hundred. My group was told to occupy the large barrack building that looked so much like a log hut.

The main gate was adorned by a large Soviet Star, made of a timber frame covered with red cloth. The cloth was a bit faded but it was unmistakably red. On either side stood two more red flags marking the corner pillars, and close by was a gatehouse with a small entrance door creaking on its hinges in the slight breeze. This was occupied by the duty guards.

Alongside this guard hut was the 'cooler', half sunk into the ground and assigned to those who, by definition and judgement of the Russian camp authorities, had either misbehaved generally, lied during interrogation, defied the usurpers or had been caught after going 'absent without leave'. Several prisoners had been incarcerated in that dreadful place.

The camp was certainly large, laid out in a square with a wide road running down the middle. To the right, when entering the camp, were four accommodation huts lined up in pairs at right angles to the roadway, each pair being separated from the other by a small square with a more modern timber house to one side. This was 'The Anti-Fascist Office', which also housed a library.

At the far end of the camp, and facing down the roadway, was the camp kitchen and a dining hall which had a small stage and also doubled as the theatre.

Over on the far side of the camp were three more timber buildings. Parallel to the roadway and set back quite a bit was one more set of PoW accommodations. At that side of the site were the administrative offices, or Kommandantur, which also housed the office of the Russian camp commander, our Wurzelzwerg and his interpreter.

The most important building of all, as it turned out, was the hospital set at the end of the Headquarters block. It was presided over by Dr Bolkova, a most remarkable, dedicated and compassionate woman who, within her capabilities, did everything possible for us.

Dr Bolkova (I never discovered her first name) was about fifty years old, an almost diminutive figure with long auburn hair which she plaited neatly, wearing it wound around her head like a crown. Always dressed in a white frock, she was to be seen everywhere her authority, and often her curiosity, should lead. I seem to remember she had the rank of colonel. Assuredly, she enjoyed considerable stature among her compatriots. Her responsibility covered everything that concerned the welfare of the PoWs, and accordingly she was in charge of hygiene, health and food. Thanks to her total incorruptibility, we received what was due to us each and every day so long as the supply lines worked.

She came up trumps during the winter. The supply of bread flour, pulses, fish and oatmeal for the inevitable kasha dried up, and as a consequence all provisions had to be rationed. However, as soon as the warehouse was restocked, she made sure personally that everything we had missed was made up to us, in addition to resuming our daily rations.   Because of Dr Bolkova, those were the days of plenty.

To overcome the innate corruptibility of Russians and to ensure that none of the civilians fed through the same warehouse could take any advantage, she put one of the German PoWs whom she trusted most, together with a couple of assistants, in charge of the warehouse. They were accountable to her and her alone.   Dr Bolkova knew full well that nobody would be able to cheat them and that even a higher ranking Russian officer trying to pull rank would be shown the door, politely but firmly.   At first, this seemed almost unbelievable. However, as you will see if you stay with my story, some two years later I experienced this same degree of trust when I was put in charge of a wages office.

As I have already said, each barrack hut could accommodate one hundred and sixty men.   As in the smaller camp there were two continuous bunks on two levels down each side of a central aisle.   It was a tight squeeze.   Allowing just fifty centimetres per person, each bunk could just provide room for forty men and, provided there were enough barrack buildings, the entire one thousand strong body of prisoners could be housed with general discomfort in one half of the camp.   But as there were only six barracks on each side of the roadway, in theory forty men would have to sleep outside.   The Russians had a simple solution, to squeeze them into the one long building lying parallel to the roadway, which had been the home of soldiers taken prisoner as long ago as 1941.   Those old timers were not very pleased with these arrangements, to put it mildly.   However, as ever, one had to manage.

Among the inmates were a handful of Italians captured at Stalingrad, but they were sent home within three months.

It is so strange how the world turns.   I met a fellow who had been in this same camp during the First World War, when he was interned with some of his colleagues from the German Embassy in Moscow.   It was he who told us our whereabouts, and that the nearest village was Yavas in the Republic of Mordvinia, a notorious region chosen by the government as the site of penal colonies and labour camps for political prisoners and dissidents banished for many, many years.

I found that some of the wooden buildings in our camp were set up before the Napoleonic Wars. Judging by messages engraved in French on the logs and beams of our quarters, French soldiers had been kept here after 1812.

As a thoroughly captive audience, we became the target for political re-education by the 'Anti-Fascist' and his support team, who had been chosen from earlier batches of PoWs for having marked Communist tendencies. Their task was to convert us from Nazism to 'the ideology that will save humanity'. Their starting premise was· that every German had been a Nazi and could easily be won over. Our teachers obviously did not appreciate the lessons we had already been learning about the Soviet Union, nor that not all German soldiers were members of the Nazi party.

These Nazi hunters were a formidable force in camp life and one had to be very careful not to let one's own feelings run high. Denunciation by the Antis, or by other prisoners, became almost routine. Files were kept on everyone and reports were passed to the Russian political commissar for his own records and appropriate action. This would lead to interrogation and, if one did not admit one's wrongdoings or bad thoughts, to being sentenced to a day or two in the cooler or assigned some unpleasant intensive labour.

Maybe I was born a cynic, but I could not help wondering whether the re-educators really believed what they preached, or had been brainwashed in the cause of a supposedly better society. I suspected that in many cases it was neither, but rather a devious way to improve their own lot. After all, their privileges were substantial. They received double rations of food, they were never required to perform physical work, they luxuriated in the warmth of their own separate hut, and stood a chance of attending a special Comintern training school, to be groomed for higher office in the new Germany where Russia would be boss.

Maybe they really did believe they had seen the true light. Certainly they were the first to be released, no doubt to prepare the ground for further infiltration and consolidation of the Communist regime before the mass of PoWs could return home.

The camp library was filled with all the books one was supposed to digest to further the cultural re-education. They ran the gamut from Stalin's speeches to the Congress of the Bolshevik Party, by way of Molotov, Machorski and Kalinin to books by Heinrich Mann, poems by Heinrich Heine and the wisdom of Karl Marx and Joseph Engels, Thälmann and Rosa Luxemburg. These, we were told, were the only true heroes the world had ever known. One book I had not expected to find was a science fiction work by Dominick, the writer of futuristic novels, all but one of whose imaginings had been transformed into fact in our own lifetime.

The book in question was entitled *The Trail of Dhingiskhan*. It was a most enthralling story about political and economic developments in Europe, which began on page one with the destruction of the Soviet Air Force by the combined West European Air Fleet over Scandinavia and the subsequent collapse of the Soviet Empire. Apart from the air battle, it was fifty years ahead of its time.

I am an avid reader, so I took full advantage of the chance to study the politics of the left in order to find out which were better, the brown shirts or the red. In the end, I tried to assess the differences between Nazi Germany and the Soviet Union. The result was very simple. There was little to choose between them in the way they sought to carry out their policies, and my view of Communism formed through my reading may be summed up totally by the expression 'during the winter it is much colder in Russia'.

They just did not stand a chance to convert me, at least, to the Red Cause. Had I been a dedicated Nazi I might have been won over, for surely it is easier to convert an ardent supporter of any faith than to sway someone like myself who thinks independently on practically everything.

No doubt my upbringing was responsible for making me such a free thinker. My father's work was closely tied to the film industry, mostly run in his early days by Jews, and I respected them for being clever, hard-working people. Nazis took a different view, maintaining that Aryans were by right superior to all, but I shared my father's opinion that men of integrity could be found in all races. We also had cause to know that not all Aryans were honourable!

Father hated being told what to do by people he despised. He was a free thinker and, by and large, his own views always appealed to him better than others'. Consequently he could not bring himself to join the Party and made sure that I, too, thought carefully about party commitments. I remember most particularly a day, when I was fifteen years old, when he took me into his study, sat me down and asked me what plans I had in mind. My school work was beginning to suffer because I was devoting too much time to the Hitler Youth Movement, but I had not worked out what I had to do.

"Son, you do not learn for the benefit of your teachers, nor for the glory of the school, and certainly not for me. Learning is completely personal. It is for your own good. School results will determine what you are able to do with your life. You can't sit back and hope that just because you were a good member of the Hitler Youth you will be able to earn enough to live on."

This advice was so obviously right that the next day I asked for my release from the Movement on the grounds that I had problems at school. They let me go willingly, for the last thing the Party would tolerate was that one of its members should become a disgrace to them by getting poor grades. I took off my uniform and never wore it again. The world outside Germany was led to believe that membership of the Party, and of its organisations, was required of all Germans, but in actual fact this was not so.

I always tended to stick to the middle of the road in politics, and by no stretch of imagination could I ever support the far left. I was certainly not alone in this and therefore was not the only anti-Communist PoW. I am quite sure it was one of us who pinned a drawing of the 'Three Wise Monkeys' (see no evil, speak no evil, hear no evil) to the Anti-Fascist notice board. The Antis were not amused, but we were!

A pleasant surprise was to find that our new accommodation was free of bed-bugs, but, as if to make up for this relief, we had to share it with big, fat rats. It is not very amusing at night to see one or more of those charming animals happily chewing away on a sock one was wearing in an attempt to keep warm, or on a bit of food put aside for a snack. Occasionally a rat would gnaw through the sock and start dining on a big toe, which was not very pleasant, either.

A council of war was called and after long deliberations it was decided to apply measures that had been tried out during the War to apparently good effect. When one of us was in the 'shoe factory' he would get a small quantity of diesel oil from the generator and smuggle it into the hut. We caught one rat alive, dipped it into the oil tail first, set it alight and released it under the floorboards, having made sure we could put out any fire that might get started as a result.

This was not sport, nor was it what one might call sporting. The screams let out by the rat were ear-piercing as it tried to run away from the fire at its tail-end. Cruel it undoubtedly was, but the treatment immediately rid us of our plague of rats, which probably moved over to neighbouring wooden huts and houses.

Camp life brought out the best and the worst in us PoWs because, in those early days at least, it was so mind-numbingly dull that one either tolerated the boredom, or got up to mischief in order to find any possible way to relieve it.

Strangely, it was under these unusual conditions, that in my own hut I managed to strike up a couple of truly remarkable friendships, the closest I ever had. In the bed space to my left had nestled down a young Navy sub-lieutenant called Wilfried, a fellow who had his feet firmly on the ground, and to my right a former artillery officer and engineer called Heinz.

We managed to stay together thereafter. During the coming years we helped each other through some of the most trying circumstances anyone could imagine, and the ties forged during those years were destined to hold for the rest of our lives. We shared everything: what was mine was theirs; what was theirs was mine. Between us everything was common property – food and clothes, and our sorrows as well. No request was ever queried, no thanks either expected or given. Ours became that true friendship where mere thanks would have been both inadequate and excessive.

The first morning after moving into the 'large' camp, we were assigned to our tasks immediately after roll-call. We were detailed off, two by two, into parties of six for tree felling or for cutting logs. Others were assigned to farm duties, like tending the cabbage and potato fields, or harvesting maize. The crops growing around us were for consumption on the camp, which was designed to be fully self-sufficient.

I always liked working with wood and was quite happy to be assigned to be a lumberjack. Heinz and Wilfried came on to the same team, together with a rather distinguished-looking fellow who, to our delight, fitted into our little group to make up a permanent fourth friend. We learned that his name was Oscar and that he was later to become the manager of a large bank in Braunschweig and, furthermore, was highly educated. In character he was much like Heinz, with whom he tended to pair off. Wilfried and I, who tended to be heavier on brawn than on brains, also paired off!

When we changed assignment from tree-felling to log cutting, it was Oscar who suggested that we resort to word games in order to keep the little grey matter alive and to ease the monotony of pulling and pushing the saws.

This was one of his problems: "Define a spiral staircase and explain without moving your arms how it goes round and round."

The best we could come up with was, "A succession of steps which lead up or down and which are arranged around a real or imagined vertical axis."

As the days went by, we settled down to a routine which seemed governed by the day of the week. Some assignments were better than others, and making sauerkraut was the most sought-after occupation. You had a chance to eat as many carrots and as much white cabbage as you liked, and smuggle some back into the camp to share with your friends.

Making sauerkraut was simple. Enormous wooden barrels, two metres or so in diameter and three metres high, had been let into the ground. Into these we threw finely chopped cabbage, carrots and the like. As a layer of vegetables was evenly laid down it was covered by a layer of salt. And then...

Some of us were kitted out with waders. We had to climb down into the barrel and stamp on the stuff being chucked down from above. When the barrel was full it was covered by a wooden lid and allowed to rest for a while. The result was sauerkraut. Why did we make so much? It was our staple diet. Sauerkraut came with everything, day in and day out, for weeks and months on end, throughout the next four years.

One day, during tree-felling, I either did not hear or ignored the warning 'Timber!' A tree came down and, looking for something to rest on comfortably, hit me on the head. Next thing I knew I was lying in bed in hospital. Apparently I had suffered concussion and was consequently out of circulation for some time. My condition seemed to give Dr Bolkova cause for concern (I was also a little worried), not simply for the knock on the head but for the fact that I had also developed sinusitis. It turned out that the hospital was particularly short on drugs, and all the doctor could arrange for me was to apply head compresses and cover the affected parts of my body with soothing, steamy towels. Shortly, however, things began to look up for us patients.

A train arrived from Breslau, full of goodies liberated from flats and houses. Mirror-fronted wardrobes and cabinets, sideboards still full of china and cutlery, a piano, linen and kitchenware, pictures, tables, chairs, carpets and hand towels. Of greater importance to the hospital, though, the shipment included the contents of a pharmacy, or in German 'Apotheke'.

There was a great variety of much needed medical goods including ointments, bandages, plaster, elastics and much more. Dr Bolkova's eyes gleamed at the sight of all the goodies and she set about sorting them out. Those of us who could leave our beds were ordered to join her in the large treatment room, where all the boxes and vials had been piled up, and were told to sort them out by name and identical appearance. She would read the description and composition on the packing and decide what the stuff could be used for. Thousands of pills had been found rolling around loose in the cattle truck and were delivered to the hospital in a bucket. There was no telling what they were so we sorted them by colour, markings and taste. The good doctor did the tasting! Those which could not be positively identified were separated into colours and pulverised for later use in dyeing material in the making of costumes for the theatre group.

With the help of aspirin and other newly acquired medications, I was able to get on my hind legs fairly quickly and return to cutting timber and making sauerkraut.

Unloading the furniture train was the basis of stories for weeks to come and, although I was not there at the time, I seem able to recount the whole episode as though I were. The main problem was that, because no ramp could be found and the cattle trucks stood about 1.5 metres above the ground, everything had to be unloaded manually. This presented real difficulties when it came to lowering the mirrored cabinets. The weight of the furniture was more than the poor PoWs could manage and, remarkably, all those pieces slipped through their hands. All the mirrors were shattered as they tumbled to the ground. There was much swearing in Russian, and German as well for good measure, but nothing could be done about it. What a shame. Some of the Russian officers had been looking forward so much to furnishing their huts with the spoils of the capitalistic world, and after all their trouble had to make do without their beautiful mirrored wardrobes. Bad luck towaritsh!

Strangely, the lads had more luck with the piano, which was manhandled off nicely in one piece and transferred to our dining hall. With the piano came sheet music and a solitary violin, whereupon the Russians decided that culture should be introduced into the daily life of their guests, and word was sent around that anyone who could play an instrument or take part in a concert party should come forward.

One piano and one violin were hardly enough to form an orchestra, and obviously we needed more instruments. The only solution was to make them, and here we struck lucky. One of the PoWs came from Mittenwald, in southern Bavaria, the centre of stringed instrument making, and it turned out that he had actually worked as a violin-maker. He soon found himself in charge of a group of handymen manufacturing string instruments from the local birch wood. Not long afterwards, he set about creating clarinets, flutes and the like, and very soon we could hear the ear-shattering attempts of a fully-fledged orchestra rehearsing works by Smetana, Kalman, Strauss and other composers.

The camp put on Kalman's operetta 'The Gypsy Princess' with great success after we discovered we had a fair selection of sopranos, baritones and tenors among us. Naturally enough, the sopranos were recruited into the female roles and, I must admit, gave an impressive performance. Evening concerts followed so that we had something to look forward to when we returned from our daily chores and had a chance to relax.

I find it incredible that we front-line troops had been ignorant about so much concerning the way in which the War had been conducted. We actually had a rude awakening in the camp when one of our number, a cultural assistant able to translate from Russian into German, began a series of news bulletins taking as his source the official Soviet daily paper *Pravda*.

The news he read out brought totally unexpected insights into developments in the world outside. We stood literally open mouthed when we heard about the creation of a United Nations organisation with its General Assembly in San Francisco; and about the establishment of a War Crimes Tribunal to try Göring, Raeder, Keitel,

Hess and almost all those former members of the German High Command who had been captured.

Having spent most of our army service at the Front, we had no idea what had been going on elsewhere in wartime Germany. Perhaps understandably, we could not grasp how military men could be tried like ordinary criminals. What crimes could have been committed in the name of Germany? We knew there were such places as concentration camps, but we had never worried too much about them and certainly did not realise that they would constitute a major element in war crimes hearings.

Our position, we felt, was clear. Like front-line soldiers on either side, we had stuck out our necks for the good of our homeland, got on with our very dangerous job and left the rest to the others. And then the interrogations began...

Every day a group of PoWs was questioned about their past: last name, first name, father's first name, date of birth of oneself, father, mother and so on. Which unit? Where in Russia had you been? Had you ever fought the partisans, demolished any people's property, and had you ever been a member of a Nazi organisation? And so on, and so on.

Because of the interrogators' astonishing ignorance, some unlucky people found themselves in a total no-win situation. A particularly bad case concerned two officers who came originally from South Africa. One of them, Lt. Klein, had been a student at the Conservatory in Breslau and was the camp piano-player. He was recognised by all as being a superb musician.

Klein was questioned, cross-examined and bullied about his relationship with the other South African. The interrogating sergeant regarded it as virtually certain that as both came from the same country, they must have met and worked closely together. It so happened that Klein hailed from Durban and the other officer from Botswana, one thousand kilometres away. Any attempt to penetrate the sergeant's thick skull and get him to understand that it would be as hard for Klein to make such a connection, for it was just like the sergeant having a Russian friend living in Siberia, was futile.

As he would not admit to knowing the other South African, Klein was put in the cooler until he changed his mind. This failed to bring success so, the following day, he was sent back to the cooler. On the third day there was a change of tactics.

What was your profession before joining the army? What, you were owner of a shop which sold a complete range of men's outfits! In one shop! Hats and suits and shirts and socks and shoes and underwear, ties and coats! You have to be a liar, because such a shop does not exist. Back into the cooler went Klein. The next day he was again asked his profession, and replied, "Men's outfitter." That was too much for the sergeant who told him bluntly that he knew how clothes were sold.

"In Russia there is one shop for shoes and one for shirts and one for trousers and one for underwear etc. That's the way, understand? No? What's your profession?"

This went on again and again until the political commissar appeared.

At long last he was able to bring this farce to an end. He decided that Klein's profession was 'Magaziner' (shop keeper) and that is how it was eventually written down on the official form.

This commissar was the one who would remain with our group until the very last day in 1949. It was he who interrogated me, but unlike the sergeant he did his job with apparent regard for my feelings. He was almost understanding, and I got the feeling that he liked me, which was good in one sense, but at the same time bad. The good part was that, over the years which followed, I never had any arguments with him; the bad was that he kept me captive as long as he possibly could, claiming that he needed my help. He repeatedly promised that I would make it home, but only on the last train, and that is exactly what happened.

At his prompting I told him how my father had advised me not to join the Nazi party.

"What a clever man," he commented.

Camp routine took over to numb the senses and it was hard to find anything happening in any one day that was either worth remembering or that seemed to have brought any ray of light to the situation. Every morning the procedure was the same. First came the wake-up call, followed by the allotment of special camp duties. I never found out how the special duties men were chosen. Help would be needed in the bathhouse, in the collection of provisions, or chopping firewood for the kitchen. The latter was much sought after, for it meant a chance to get an extra helping from any leftovers in the pot. These chores were usually allocated for a month at a time.

Job allocation was followed by the counting of inmates after we had lined up on the roadway, in fives for easier numbering. The results were noted on a wooden board for, as you will remember, no paper could be spared for such records. Once the figures had been totted up and found to be correct, they were scrubbed off the wood with a piece of glass. This ceremony was followed by the most important event of the morning: breakfast. As always, this consisted of a piece of bread and kasha, which stopped the tummy rumbling for a short while. Then we went off to work until the next high point of the day, at noon, when the soup wagon would turn up at the work site and we got our soup and another small piece of bread. Soup and kasha, together with a third piece of bread, were served in the evening. We came to look on our accommodation as a sort of Bed and Breakfast with half-board!

A very few events stood out, mainly arising from our bulletins of translated Russian news. There was, for instance, the time when we learned that the Americans had dropped an atom bomb on Hiroshima and, shortly after, that Japan had surrendered. We also learned that the Soviet Union had joined in the war against Japan, by marching over the border into Manchuria immediately after the War had ended.

We were told that Japan's surrender was the direct result of Russia's involvement, and the atom bomb was just the full stop at the end of the sentence. "Glorious heroes of the Soviet Union forces brought Japan to her knees."

Did they think anyone would fall for that?

Understandably, there was much talk in the news about rebuilding a non-fascist Germany and of how the good old fatherland was to be carved up. Not all the good deeds were taking place in the eastern part of the country, we were told in passing. The rest of the land was occupied by the Western Allies who were working hand in hand with the mighty Soviet Union, in Germany and on the Security Council of the UN. I think most of us recognised the cant for what it was, but one thing we did find surprising was that the Ukraine and the Soviet Union had separate representatives at the UN, as though the Ukraine were not part of the Soviet Union.

Surprisingly, there was no work on Sundays so we could socialise with our fellows anywhere in the camp and exchange thoughts about our prospects. Except that, one Sunday a tiny figure strolled into the camp, dressed in an army greatcoat at least one size too big, which made him look even more diminutive than he really was. He disappeared into the Anti-Fascist hut and emerged shortly afterwards with the Anti Boss himself. The gong rang (that is, he hit a suspended piece of railway track with an iron rod), and word was passed around that all officers should assemble in the dining hall. So we gently strolled in, sat down at the tables and wondered what important revelations were about to be made.

In came the gnome, opened the coat and sat on top of a table, beckoning us to come closer and not to be shy. He introduced himself in fluent and accent-free German.

"My name is Engel (Angel) and I have been ordered to talk to you about Communism and bring home to you what a marvellous invention it is. After all, Communism was born in the brain of a German, Karl Marx, and we all know what clever chaps the Germans are." He told us he came originally from the Sudetenland, that strip of land along the northern boundaries of Czechoslovakia which had been handed to that newly formed republic after the First World War, and had a predominantly more German population.

I suspect that most of us were ready, at this point, to boot him out of the dining hall. Of German extraction he might be, but we could do without instruction from a Communist German. For some reason, though, we let him carry on and as a result, had a truly entertaining time.

It seems that he had been overwhelmed by Karl Marx's theories and could see their immense value to future generations. He was also inspired by the revolutionary changes being brought about in Russia, along with Lenin's own leadership. Further yet, he felt in tune with the extermination of capitalists and kulaks, the blood suckers of the peasants. This had led to him deciding, in 1928, to emigrate, to join the Bolsheviks and become a convinced political force in the workers' paradise.

"Well," he said, "I did not quite make it."

The intervening years had brought him much disquiet and so many negative experiences that he no longer believed Communism was right... and this was the man whose job, it seemed, was to preach the Soviet cause. How come?

He had found himself on the wrong side of Party doctrine and was obliged to live out his wretched life in our locality, banished from participating in the achievements of the Red community. By indoctrinating us PoWs, he had been told, he would gain a chance to redeem himself. However, as he could not care less what happened to him, he would now tell us about Communism from his strictly personal point of view.

"Listen, children," he began, "you must know that Communism is the best thing in the world; or more to the point, it would be the best thing since the invention of bread, if each human being were an angel. I do not mean that the world should be like me, Engel, but rather like the real angels who live in heaven and have wings. But we all know, they are not. I will explain."

"Take a piece of good agricultural land, erect a fence all round and divide it into two equal plots, all neatly fenced off from each other. Now go out into the big wide world and select two human beings at random. One from here," he stretched out his skinny right arm, plucking from the air an imaginary figure, "and one from there," stretching out the other arm and getting another imaginary figure. "Drop them on to their allotted piece of land, where we have provided each of them with a hut, an easy chair in which to rest their tired limbs, gardening equipment, a water supply and seeds for planting crops."

"Watch how each one sets about his job, ploughs the ground, plants the seeds and hopes for the best. As in real life, one of them is industrious whereas the other one is a lazy lout. The industrious one waters his fields, weeds his growing crop and makes sure that his garden is well tended. The other one sits all day long in his easy chair, doesn't give a damn about his plants, does not water them and simply lets the lord provide."

"Come harvest time, the lazy one looks out at high weeds and reaps meagre crops from his even more meagre efforts. He has small potatoes, green shrivelling tomatoes, not much maize and lice-infected grapes."

"His neighbour, however, has a beautiful harvest with good healthy crops, and much to show for all his efforts. Come market day, they both set off for the nearby village to sell whatever they have got. The lazy chap sells very little, and he gets next to nothing by the end of the day. His opposite number, however, sells everything and ends up with many roubles."

"They both go home and as the sun sets they settle down in front of their huts, in their easy chairs, and count their money. Stretching his legs, and green with envy about his neighbour's proceeds, Mr Lazy steps to the fence, points a finger at him and shouts, 'Hey, you capitalist!'"

Engel stopped, looked at us with his kind face and sad eyes, and brought his lesson to an end.

"Now you know why Communism won't work and why I am in this godforsaken place." He slid from the table, walked out of the door, walked down the road and disappeared out of our lives. He was a sad, disillusioned figure, betrayed by what he had honestly believed in when he was young and full of enthusiasm. His lecture was the first one about Communism I had ever attended. There was no need to go to another.

Every month we had a medical examination as Dr Bolkova had to assess each PoW for his 'fitness for employment'. One was weighed, got one's bottom pinched to see how much usable meat was left on the bones and, by pressing on the shin of the legs, whether malnutrition had already progressed so far that water had settled in the limbs and dystrophy was at an advanced stage. General appearance, injuries as a result of war wounds and so on, were all noticed and meticulously entered in individual records.

Everyone was classified, on a scale of one to four, which determined the class of work we could undertake. Categories One and Two could be employed on anything, Three on light work only, while those in Category Four, the really badly off, were restricted to complete rest and additional food (two kashas instead of one, as if that would have made much difference).

Rumour had it that there was another reason for the medical examination: to help the commission which was expected to sort out those who could work in a more severe environment, as opposed to those who were physically unsuited to helping Russia recover from the War, and who could therefore be sent home.

Dr Bolkova's entire behaviour showed her sympathy for us, particularly towards those who were obviously wounded or unfit to the point where they should go back to Germany. I remember one case especially, a man with a dreadful shrapnel wound in his back. He had a huge hole just under his shoulder blades, but apparently no internal injuries affecting his strength and health in any way. According to Dr Bolkova, he was seriously ill and she had him hospitalised shortly before the commission arrived. She told them that this man was clearly of no use to the Soviet authorities.

She managed to separate a few of those whose wounds made them look pretty awful and get them on to the repatriation list for the transport that left in November. She lied like a trooper in the face of the commission, without batting an eyelid. I wonder whether she was found out later, fell into disgrace and suffered from her masters in Moscow. I hope sincerely that this remarkable, caring woman was able to survive without trouble.

At the end of January 1946 another train arrived, this time with about two hundred Japanese PoWs who caused a commotion, which left the Russians wondering what to do. They were housed in the smaller camp, and when it came time for the Soviet soldiers to search their belongings, they made it very clear that neither the Japanese officers nor their subordinates would permit the Russians to touch any of their belongings or lay a finger on themselves. To be taken prisoner was bad enough, but it was a double indignity for this to happen after the end of the War. In their eyes the Russians were cowards, and their culture would not allow them to deal with cowards.

It seemed to the Russian commander that the obvious first step would be to call upon the services of Germany, the former Japanese ally, so he sent over to our camp to recruit a dozen or so to carry out the search.

Somehow, I came to be selected as one of the ten men for the job. This happened one Sunday, a rest day you may remember, when working parties were not to be recruited except in an emergency. Imagine our astonishment when we arrived in their camp to see all those Japanese lined up in the yard. We felt, and knew we looked, pretty scruffy by any standard; in comparison with the Japanese we must have looked disgraceful, for they were as spick and span as if they had just marched off a parade ground. Their uniforms were immaculate and their white shirts sparkled. Their officers wore shiny light brown riding boots. In a word, their appearance was impressive and in such stark contrast to the drab gear of both the Russians and the PoWs that it seemed they were from a different world. These were not fighting soldiers captured on the battlefield: one felt they had been taken prisoner as they readied themselves to march home.

There they stood, in close formation, heads up, and looking right through their sentries. Officers were at attention, three paces in front of the rank and file. Our interpreter explained to us that we were to take over what was normally the task of our guards and, with the help of another interpreter, the Russians informed the Japanese commanding officer of their intention, and met with no objection on his part.

We formed one line, each four paces apart. Upon the command of the Japanese in charge of the proceedings, each line in turn stepped forward to be subjected to the indignity of a personal search. We were warned not to touch any personal belongings and reminded that we were only there to look for foodstuffs.

The Russians must have been totally unprepared for the Asian intake and had no idea of how to cope with their diet, as rice and tins of fish were quickly put to one side. Each soldier, when under scrutiny, would sit cross-legged in front of us, totally motionless with head bowed. We felt sorry for them really and, in order to show our sympathy, put everything non-edible back neatly into the rucksacks. Now and again, when we came upon a bar of chocolate, the Japanese encouraged us with a flicker of the eyes to make the odd one disappear into our tunics, something we gratefully accepted. As there was only one guard present, such understanding between former allies passed unnoticed. Nobody searched us when we returned to our own camp.

The Japanese would not accept any orders given by the Russians and would obey only their own officers. What a difference between them and us. On one side the demoralised remnants of a once-disciplined and well trained army, and here equally defeated men who nonetheless remained proud and dignified. Of course, they had not only managed to keep their motherland, but were still able to honour their God Emperor. They occupied the camp for only two days, after which they apparently went to another camp further to the west. We never saw them again.

Back in our quarters, we shared with our friends the goodies we had picked up from the Japanese and had a real Sunday feast.

A month later the Italians were sent home and the long-expected Health Commission arrived. The inspection began early in the morning, so that by afternoon the good bodies had been sorted out from the bad ones. A few days later the Category Four men were handed new, or at least clean and presentable, clothes and bade the rest of us farewell. Presumably they made their way back home, though no one actually confirmed this.

We were allowed to grow our hair again, a sign that winter was approaching. In fact it came early that year, with a severity that reminded us very much of the winter of 1941/42. Snow quickly settled on the ground, trees and the roofs of our huts and transformed the dreary squalor into a fairy-tale landscape. At the same time we were issued with winter clothing: thick, quilted jackets and trousers, felt boots and gloves. We were also given warm hats, some of genuine rabbit skin (for the hierarchy), while those destined for us ordinary workers were of simulated fur.

The huts were now heated all day long by large wood-burning stoves. A fire-fighting troop was on guard twenty-four hours a day, safety being the order of the day. Outdoor activities were not curtailed, though, and after roll-call every morning we trundled off into the woods to fell and chop. Days were noticeably shorter and the morning counting was delayed by an hour or two, usually at sunrise. I stood in line with one of my nearest 'neighbours' on the bunk, a tall artist with a deep voice and a magnificent beard on which the snow flakes settled to turn him into a real Father Christmas. As the sun began to rise, it cast rays across the roofs to paint the snow in shades of blue and purple, lilac, mellow green and gold.

"Look at the snow," my friend said, "and when we artists paint lilac snow we are told that our impression is wrong. Snow has to be white. Look at it, there is lilac snow. The difference is that we artists see the things as they are, and are they not beautiful?"

That artist certainly opened my eyes.

As religious festivals were not on the Soviet agenda we correctly assumed that there would be no day off for Christmas, so we decided to celebrate on the following Sunday. We were determined to do the utmost to mark the occasion. The theatre group had been rehearsing the operetta 'Die Fledermaus' and there were a couple of orchestral performances organised as well. Accustomed to enjoying whatever was on offer as a break in the daily routine, we looked forward to these cultural treats.

The kitchen had a surprise in store as well. For weeks they had squirrelled away provisions – no easy task to escape discovery in any one of the many Russian inspections. There was a standing order that any food coming into the camp had to be used to the last crumb, but somehow our cook managed to produce some sort of cake. Where he got the sugar from, better not to know, but it made it something special and was appreciated by all us PoWs.

That Sunday I visited some of the PoWs I had got to know particularly well, and who lived in the admin block where the old hands had made themselves very comfortable indeed. For instance, they had replaced the continuous bunk beds with single bunks in pairs, and had small tables set against the windows to make it possible to look out on to the square and watch the world go by. One of those lucky inmates was an army chaplain, who had served on the staff of Field Marshal Schörner when he headed the last of the 5th Army in Czechoslovakia. He was an impressive character, tall and with a thunderous voice that could fill a cathedral. He still wore his uniform, surprisingly. He also had a cross dangling from his neck, tucked away out of sight most of the time, along with his wristwatch. How he had managed to hang on to those treasures despite all the frisking he, and all the rest of us, had suffered, beats me.

However, we sat on his bunk and were talking about the good old days, what culinary treats mother had produced for the festive season, and how delightful it had been to have one's family gathering under the Christmas tree during those peaceful days before the carnage began. Inevitably we were soon talking about the years from 1933 on, the resistance and the claims by so many of Hitler's followers that they had neither been true supporters of the Nazis, nor ever voted for them, and had been always opposed to them. I often wondered how it was that a ninety percent vote was cast when so many opposed putting Hitler into the saddle!

It was hardly surprising that he won so much support from a people who had been humiliated by the Versailles Treaty, and were suffering the worst economic crisis they had ever known. They would have clutched at any straw that would help them climb out of the mud. The emerging Nazi Party promises had been matched by deeds, so that many doubters were won over by what they saw as the sincerity of the new leadership. Others retained their doubts, but were prepared to go along with the new regime, although some would not be convinced and said as much. Before long they wound up in political concentration camps, mainly Oranienburg, near Berlin.

My father, who was adamantly anti-Nazi, was in a circle of friends, Jewish and non-Jewish, who had favoured the former Weimar Republic. But with the rise of Nazism, Jews found themselves ostracised, while political free thinkers were chased out of the country. Consequently both groups were desperate for help. Because, through his business, my father had built up connections in foreign countries, he was able to help a great many of his closest friends to escape to England. With great good fortune, he managed to maintain a fairly low profile and escaped being arrested, although he was at one time interrogated by members of the Gestapo, suspicious that so many of his closer acquaintances were disappearing.

He actually developed a quite extensive network of spies and so was able to get prior warning of when the authorities were about to make an 'unexpected' visit. Word came through that Triviranus, one of his closest friends and the last Minister of Post and Telecommunications in the Weimar Government, was about to be arrested, so Father went to Wiesbaden and without ceremony led him from the tennis court out to the airport, and put him on a plane to

England. Triviranus was still in his tennis gear when he arrived in London, broke but happy. My father was concerned as to how he would be able to survive in Britain without any funds and got over this problem by resorting to smuggling. He had to fly over on business from time to time, to call on Rank Studios, and took the opportunity to line his underwear with cash which he handed over personally to his friend. In due course Triviranus got on his feet and was able to support himself, whereupon Father looked for another needy cause.

All this I told my chaplain friend in the camp. He embraced me and, turning to the others with tears bursting from his eyes, declared that he knew my story was true from personal experience.

"This is the son of the one man who I will have to thank for ever for helping Triviranus, my closest friend and comrade in arms during the First World War. That help enabled him to escape and, despite the great dangers that were ever present, enabled him to build a new life abroad."

I felt humble, but at the same time somewhat relieved to come across such startling confirmation of my father's unblemished behaviour in those years. This story eventually filtered through to the Anti-Fascist Group in our camp and as a result seems to have improved my standing. Whenever I went to the library I was treated with much kindness, and I was, thankfully, never asked to become allied to the Anti-Fascist Group.

As 1945 turned into the new year, there was such a hard frost that we had to stay in camp for a couple of weeks and, with nothing to keep us occupied, we soon missed the daily work and spent far too much time thinking about food.

Suddenly it was spring. Wild flowers shot through the undergrowth and nature turned green again. According to our masters, winter finished on the first day of April, on which day we had to hand in our heavy clothes and make do with the ordinary Russian uniforms.

Exactly two weeks later, the usual hammering of the 'gong' announced that my twenty-fifth birthday had come along, and for a present I was assigned by chance to the kitchen firewood chopping party. This meant I would have plenty to eat, not simply on my birthday, but for the next four weeks.

I could not have been more wrong! That turned out to be the most miserable birthday ever. For some reason I never managed to discover, there was not enough food on hand to permit anything but the minimum of rations for everyone in camp. Later that day, though, I had some good news in the shape of my first letter from home, so hopefully the world would look better from then on.

Confinement in Lager 58 neared its end. The first anniversary of our being taken prisoner went by, but then, towards the middle of May, preparations began for the dissolution of the camp. One by one the individual barrack members were called up and assigned to their cattle trucks, and an engine was hooked on to haul the train away.

When the gate opened for our group we were counted yet again and all were found to be present and correct, so we were told to climb into our cattle trucks, forty to each one, and with much jolting and crashing we began the next stage of our journey. This time the locomotive pulled us north, in effect heading in the same direction that we had been following when we had arrived at the camp.

As we began to gather speed I looked back and saw the lonely figure of Dr Bolkova, hands buried in her white dress, watching the wagonloads of 'her' PoWs disappearing into the birch tree wilderness. Was she to have a new assignment, too? I hoped the future would be kind to her. She deserved the best.

That's what was left of Schörner's Army (top)

First interrogation (bottom)

A bit of relaxation (top)

Anti-fascist Activist addresses camp inmates (bottom)

9th May 1945   On the road from Prague (top)

Settling down by the roadside (bottom)

One side the Russians, the other the POWs (top)

Through Constanta (bottom)

81

СОЮЗ ОБЩЕСТВ КРАСНОГО КРЕСТА и КРАСНОГО ПОЛУМЕСЯЦА СССР

Почтовая карточка военнопленного
Carte postale du prisonnier de guerre

Bespiatno
Franc de post

Кому (Destinataire) *Heinz Apel*

Куда (Adresse) *(15) Döllstedt*
(страна, город, улица, № дома, округ, село, деревня)
Kr. Gotha

Отправитель (Expéditeur)
Фамилия и имя военнопленного
Nom du prisonnier de guerre

Почтовый адрес военнопленного
Adresse du prisonnier de guerre
Lager 7564

тип. Зак. 395

Издательство
«СОВЕТСКИЙ
ХУДОЖНИК»

К 25-летию
ОТКРЫТОЕ ПИСЬМО
пионерской организации

Куда ГЕРМАНИЯ
Russ. Zone (15)
Döllstädt / Kr. Gotha

Кому
Herrn
Heinz Apel

Адрес отправителя
SSSR.

8 сентября 1932 года врагами советского народа убит Павлик Морозов — председатель совета пионерского отряда в селе Герасимовке, на Урале Павлик бесстрашно разоблачал кулаков, которые мешали организовать колхоз. Каждый юный ленинец будет свято хранить память о славном пионере—герое Павлике Морозове.

7. «Павлик Морозов»

А-08604. Тираж 80.000. Заказ 594.
21-я тип. им. Ивана Федорова треста «Полиграфкнига» ОГИЗа при Совете Министров СССР.
Ленинград. Звенигородская, 11.

A Postcard to Heinz

TEMPORARY PROMOTION

When you are cooped up in a cattle truck, one train journey is very much like any other. You lose track of time, which is perhaps merciful for, by not worrying about things over which you have no control, you feel more likely to stay sane. The highlight of our journey from Yavas, then, was when it came to an end alongside a loading ramp at a largish rail yard. We transferred to waiting lorries and, leaving the yard, I glimpsed the station sign, which read 'LOPASAIA'.

As usual, we went nowhere near the town centre and were only able to see the outskirts – rows and rows of depressingly ugly, tall forbidding blocks in obvious need of a paint and plaster job. We passed a direction sign to Moscow over on the right and, as it turned out, we were in fact only thirty kilometres away from the Soviet capital. The road we were on turned out to be the main link between Moscow and Tula and led eventually to Charkov.

Leaving the built-up area of Lopasaia we came to countryside, mostly fields interspersed with spinners. Alongside the road, on our right, ran a railway main line with passenger and goods trains thundering along in both directions. The passenger coaches were crowded, with a fair number of people sitting on the roofs of the carriages, variously clutching pieces of luggage, baskets and even small animals. I looked wistfully at those trains, wishing that I could be on one, going home.

A long industrial complex came into view, with a large, barren field dominated by a huge oak tree. A railway line from the factory crossed this field and swept in an arc, right across the main road, to terminate in a yard that was dominated by a large stone-crushing machine, a cement silo and a bulk concrete mixer. These very noisy and dusty pieces of equipment seemed to be set up solely to service road construction, there being nothing else likely to take its output for as far as we could see in any direction.

We turned in to the left and pulled up by the gate of a tented camp, set parallel to the road and very close to it. Four tents, each designed to hold forty men, were lined up next to each other at right angles to the fenced-off road, while a fifth tent closed the rear and housed the administration. At right angles to this again was an ablution tent beyond which was another tent complex set aside for food storage and cooking. This was to be our new home, for a while at least.

Forty at a time, we were detailed off to the tents and found that each one had been floored with a thick layer of straw. Blankets laid on the straw marked off each PoW's bed space.

Our guards also slept under canvas, in another tented site some fifty metres away.

We made ourselves at home and took a look round our new holiday camp to see how it compared with what we had experienced elsewhere. That evening came the inevitable roll-call after which we were told precisely what we were expected to do. As I had thought, we had been sent there to rebuild a section of the main road. Our bit, apparently, extended to ten kilometres and filled in a gap that had been left by other working parties who had completed stretches of road on either side of ours.

We were assembled into three working parties, two small and one large. One was to man the stone crushing plant and concrete mixer, another (the large group) would do the actual road building, and the remaining group was to stay ready for a special job about which we would learn more in due time. I was put in charge of that group. As the Russian word for such groups means 'brigade', I found myself promoted to the rank of 'brigadier'!

The following morning, after again being counted to make sure that no one had fallen by the wayside, the first and second groups left camp. My group stood around hoping for the best and fearing the worst. Before long, though, a jovial civilian turned up and had a pow-wow with our camp commandant, a major. Our interpreter explained to me that we would have to go with this civilian to the munitions factory in the background, as we had been given the task of digging a trench for the district heating system – a system of producing heat in a central boiler house and piping steam or hot water to various buildings within a given area.

Our civilian natschalnik and I walked in front, with the rest of my group following along on their own, for this was the first time that we had been allowed out without guards! They must really trust us a lot, I thought.

There was one slight problem. I did not speak Russian, nor did my new superior speak German, and the interpreter was miles away. But in no time at all I managed to understand from his hand-waving and finger pointing what was required, and to make quite sure he sketched out a simple drawing in the sand. I put it all into German, and off we all went to work.

A team from our kitchen arrived on the scene at around noon, with our ration of soup and bread, but the soup was some sort of mouldering plant thrown into boiling water and was well nigh inedible. One of our group thought that it might be nettle soup, while another said it was more like garbage stew. Well, we had no option but to eat the stuff, as it was clear that we would get nothing else. That evening, after following our civilian friend back to the camp, we had the same pretence of a meal. It suddenly dawned on me that we were now in the hands of the Red Army and not the KGB. The outlook was not good.

In charge of provisions was a miserable, unpleasant, thoroughly disagreeable gnome of a Russian sub-lieutenant. At all times he wore his peaked cap on the back of his head. His legs were as bent as two bananas and he seemed to sag in an army uniform two sizes too big for him. This unappetising representative of the Red Army went to town twice a week to fetch general provisions, and three times a week to get bread. We found that our bread portions were smaller than they used to be, and upon close examination discovered that we were getting about fifty grams less per portion than we were supposed to.

There was never any meat, nor fish, nor sugar, nor pulses. If there was ever a clear case of cheating and corruption, this was it. We discovered all the gory details surprisingly quickly.

The provisions were usually collected by an army truck with our diminutive sub-lieutenant in attendance. However, one time a civilian lorry was used and the driver told us afterwards what was going on. After collecting all the food we were entitled to at the magazine (store), he had to drive his load directly to the black market where everything, apart from the bread, was sold. Then dry nettles were obtained as substitute food for the hungry prisoners. The ill-gotten gain was rapidly turned into vodka or some other spirit. We could do nothing about it, at least for the moment. Worst of all, our own little Russian officer was always so drunk he was what armies everywhere refer to as 'pissed as a newt'.

Close to where my group and I worked was a small stream. A jetty built with large, flat rocks all around was the local laundry and every day it would be used by women of all ages, from young teens to quite old, who would chatter and laugh while they washed the dirty linen the ancient way, by beating the clothes with small flat stones and splashing them on the large rocks with copious quantities of water. Soap was not to be had for laundering, so the dirt was removed by a combination of brute force and flowing water. The scene was reminiscent of paintings portraying women washing their garments in the eighteenth century.

Mind you, it was hard to hear their chatter even though they were so near. All pleasant noises were swamped by the continuous blaring of loudspeakers, for ever exhorting the workers to greater output. It seems that these mind-destroying loudspeakers were used everywhere in the Soviet Union as part of a serious campaign of brainwashing.

Someone must have decreed that the volume had to be as high as possible, regardless of distortion, and at all hours the air was poisoned with stirring songs about Mother Russia, or extracts from speeches by Lenin, Stalin and other Party chiefs, or with standard quotations and resolutions in praise of the working classes and the undefeatable Soviet nation. Many of the sayings condemned capitalists, or called for pledges to raise work standards and the quality of life by following the Party line. For good measure there were reminders to exceed the minimum quota in honour of various days of remembrance, such as 'Red Army Day' or the 'Day of the Congress of the glorious Bolshevik Party', or the commemoration of the October Revolution, and so on.

The texts were also to be seen on large red banners strung across streets and along the sides of every conceivable building. On the second day of our trench digging exercise, my friendly boss pulled me into his office and produced a Russian-German dictionary, which, he managed to explain, he had 'borrowed' from his son, whose first foreign language at school was German. A smile lit up his furrowed face, and after referring to his acquisition, he strung together a sentence to the effect that from now on we would converse in both languages. He would learn some German, and I some Russian. In next to no time we were talking in a simplified infinitive version of the other's language.

It was then that I discovered, among other things, that the Russian alphabet does not know an 'H' and substitutes this with a 'G', so not surprisingly I went through the rest of my time in Russia under the name 'Gans' instead of Hans!

Close by was a garage and, whenever I had the opportunity, I mixed with the drivers and listened to their conversation, memorising words and repetitive expressions. In the evening I would ask our camp interpreter what they meant, and within a short time I discovered that Russian was governed by a far more complicated grammar than any I had studied before. There are actually five official cases (plus one unofficial one, the case of incessant uncertainty!).

The days went by, the weather was warm and sunny and we had no complaints apart from the wretched food. Bath day came around once a week, on Saturday, in a communal bathhouse/delousing station some two kilometres away from our camp. We were each given a piece of soap and allowed to splash about with plenty of hot water. After drying off we put on clean underwear.

Unfortunately, we were not allowed to keep a spare pair of underpants and vest, and as we were also not able to have a decent wash during the week, everyone truly looked forward to the Saturday outing. During our absence from camp, as one might have expected, our belongings were searched and everything that could be construed as a means of aiding an escape attempt (even such a paltry item as a piece of bread one had saved for an evening snack) was confiscated. The soldiers must have had even less to eat than us, it seemed.

Working steadily at the trench-building job there came a time, of course, when we finished and were given a new assignment. This involved sitting by the roadside and splitting rocks. Have you ever tried to split a granite rock and decimate it into small chippings with nothing more powerful than a hand-held hammer? Take my word for it – you get mad from frustration, for there is no way you can succeed.

We were not alone in our reconstruction work. There were also civilians, who had to earn their daily bread by doing the same work that we did. The difference was that they had to work to their 'norm'. I do not remember how many cubic metres – or more likely, cubic centimetres – they had to produce each day, but they had got the hang of splitting rocks. Where we were hitting like mad with large mallets or small hammers, letting off steam all the time, they looked at their own rock, took a small hammer and, hey presto, split it into two or three parts. Natural pride prevented us allowing them to do it when we could not, so there was nothing for it but to consult these specialists. They showed us how to read the veining of the stone and split it with a light stroke at the right spot. It did not work all the time, but we soon got the hang of it, and even small progress was some progress. If all the work was done by hand, why had the Russians put up that monster of a stone crusher? Anyway, the heaps of rock got smaller and we envisaged that this form of slavery would soon come to an end.

About two kilometres from our camp was the edge of a large wood, which ran parallel to the road for quite some while and served as a screen for a military airfield from which, mostly on Tuesdays and

Thursdays, aircraft would take off for exercises. Most of the planes were two-seater PL 12s, very similar to our own Messerschmitt 110. Among us were two Luftwaffe officers who found it necessary to do their 'business' rather frequently in the wood. They always went alone, not wishing to inconvenience their comrades or the guards, and always went as far as permissible, without arousing suspicion. In the evenings they stuck their heads together. We were naturally curious, but knew better than to ask embarrassing questions. On Thursday the PL 12s apparently went on long-distance exercises, and on Thursdays, too, our two flyers got very itchy feet. But nothing happened for a while. Then one day, halfway through the morning, we were herded together and counted. One of their planes was missing and so were our two escapees. Obviously, they had dared to take the Russian aircraft. Should they be caught, we were reminded, they would be sent right back to us, for the procedure was that whoever escaped and was caught had to be returned to the place from whence he came. Not a great deal would happen then though, apart from getting a good dressing-down and a few days in the cooler. Afterwards, any escapees were usually put in a position of trust, no doubt on the basis that, if they were clever enough to hit the road, they must possess qualities which were much in demand by the Soviet authorities!

Anyway, on the day of the airmen's escape we found ourselves back in the camp in next to no time, and were counted again and again until everyone was dead sure that we definitely were two down on strength. All afternoon each man was interrogated, with special attention being paid to the leaders of the working brigades. This went on well into the night, but to no avail. Even if one of us had known anything we would not have said a word, despite threats to transfer us to a penal battalion. We knew that summary 'execution' was just not on in the circumstances.

Interrogations continued the following day, Friday, with additional Russian personnel being brought in and the guard strengthened. Who could blame the camp authorities? The remaining Germans might escape next time, perhaps by U-Boat down the little stream by the munitions factory.

That Saturday there was no bathing.

Sunday was fairly quiet, if one ignored our camp commandant's frequent calls for a roll-call. He threatened to string us up from the big oak tree in front of the camp if he failed to get to the bottom of the affair.

He got his revenge that evening, when a train pulled into the siding, loaded with granite rocks in fifty ton cattle trucks. How the rock got into the trucks in the first place, heaven knows.

We were called out to unload the trucks. Apart from the inherent difficulties of getting the granite out through the truck doors, I could see that it could be somewhat dangerous. Nonetheless, we managed to complete the task without any serious injuries, although it was past midnight when we finally got back to our tents and were able to take a rest.

The following morning we went to work as usual. I had been instructed to prepare a section of the road for the following day's work but, as the normal work parties were still engaged on their own activity, we could actually achieve very little, and it was not until late in the afternoon that we could get under way in earnest. One by one the individual parties finished their jobs and walked back to camp, until we were the only brigade still on the road. Our young soldier guard was bored stiff and began to become rather tetchy, trying to push us along. I told him to keep quiet and wait until I gave the order to return to the camp. He saw this as some sort of insubordination and pulled out his bayonet and hit me with it on the left upper arm. Without stopping to think, I saw red and hit him right across his face, almost expecting him to pull the trigger. To my surprise nothing happened. He must have remembered that there were two things he was not allowed to do: interfere with our work and/or give any instructions; and hit a PoW, let alone an officer. He stepped back, his face drawn and angry, but made no further attempt to force us back to the camp.

When eventually we returned to camp, I immediately reported the incident to both the Russian camp commandant and the political officer. They said not a word and only pointed to the main gate from whence our guard appeared with his commanding officer. His account of the affair was identical with mine, and the only action taken, to my great surprise and relief, was that I was demoted, lost my group leader status and had to return to the ranks to split stones. Why my dear friend Wilfried was also punished as a result of my encounter, and also lost his job remains a mystery to this day.

A few days later we were called out in the late afternoon to unload a consignment of loose cement which, once again, had been loaded into cattle trucks. This was about the worst job I was to experience during my entire time in Russia. We had no protective clothing and wore just a shirt and a pair of trousers, and had to wade in the cement and unload it as best we could through the door and the windows.

Cement dust and sweat do not go together, and very soon I looked like a Greek marble statue, only not as pretty. Eyes, ears and nose were filled with the filthy grey stuff while the feeling of caked cement on the skin was simply indescribable. After hours of huffing and puffing, we got the job done. The wagons were empty and the cement was lying on the raised embankment, held back from cascading down the slope by the wall of rocks which we had unloaded a few days earlier.

Back home we went. All we could do was use the water hose to clean us and our clothes as best we could. Luckily enough it was still very warm at night and by the morning we were almost dry. Anything that started off damp first thing would definitely dry off as we wore it. We had most assuredly become quite resilient.

We PoWs were making the best of things, but we had really had a gutful of being pushed around. Then came Changeover Friday. I will never forget it in my whole life.

A commission of inspectors arrived and toured the site. They were at the crusher compound, talking to some of the PoWs, when the lunch time soup barrels arrived. Even on this day we were to get the same grey-green concoction as always, and without stopping to think, all the frustration of living in that dreadful camp burst right out. One of our number started shouting at the Russian officers and all hell broke loose. The soup was thrown on the ground in front of them and one inmate after another complained in very precise terms about the conditions under which we had to live.

Remember, we were under a Red Army administration in this camp. The members of the commission were KGB officers. Their faces turned to stone and they ordered an immediate halt to all work and had us taken back to camp.

No sooner had we gone though the gate than the provision lorry drove into the compound and came to a halt by the kitchen. Out of the driver's cabin reeled the sub-lieutenant, drunk as ever, who leant against the door of the kitchen and gargled, "I want my bread," unaware that the head of the commission was standing right next to him. We needed no further back-up for our story. The KGB commissioner grabbed the little squirt by his collar and, with us looking on, dragged the pathetic little bundle through the dust to the gate-house. There he pushed the door open and he threw him into the far corner. Our former guardian slumped against the wall, uttering not a sound.

After examining the logbook and reading the entry about my slogging match, the commissioner called me over, got me to repeat my story and declared that I could count myself lucky to be still alive. Not every soldier would have reacted as had my adversary. I apologised, but sought to justify my action by saying that it was an instant reflex and most certainly not intended to offend the Red Army or insult the Soviet Union.

Funny people these Russians; I was reinstated as group leader and so was Wilfried.

The next day KGB staff arrived to take over as camp officers; we went bathing again, and from that day on the food was all right and we had no further cause to complain.

We learned nothing about our fledglings. If they had taken the shortest and safest route to freedom, they would probably have gone north-west into Lithuania, where the locals had a well known aversion to anything Russian. Their chance of being hidden indefinitely would have been extremely good there.

Another trainload of rocks arrived and was unloaded at night, followed by another consignment of cement which we were also called out to unload. Dark clouds were banking up from the horizon as strong portents of forthcoming rain. Someone pointed out to the civilian in charge of the roadworks that the wise thing to do would be to wait until the rain had gone or the cement, shovelled on to the mass of rock lying down the embankment, would turn into a solid block. But to no avail. Rain or no rain, the train had to be unloaded as the wagons were needed elsewhere.

Of course, we were only lowly PoWs. It's your funeral, sir; we do as we are told.

Unloading began and finished without a hitch and we returned to the camp. Half an hour later the heavenly sluices opened. It rained all that night and throughout the following day. Then the sun shone again and completed the job which we had begun. No anti-tank emplacement could have been more solid than that railway embankment!

There was much scratching of heads. On this occasion we were able to hear all those delightfully expressive swear words which the Russian language has to offer, but all the swearing in the world would make not an iota of difference to the situation. Eventually we road construction specialists were called on for ideas. The solution lay in the form of a quarry in Lopasaia. Why had one not thought about that one before? Perhaps because the quarry could not be moved close to the crusher, or more likely because the whole business of quarrying stone and getting it to the site demanded something more sophisticated, like transport. Ah yes, transport was the word. Two days later, five lorries arrived with drivers, and a lorry park was set up, complete with petrol depot. Finally, a fence was set up around it for good measure.

This happened on a Sunday. Five figures walked across the road into the camp and reported to the offices. The whistle blew and we were ordered to assemble on the parade ground. The camp commandant appeared and asked, "Who is a specialist, and has a driving licence?"

Now here was a tricky question. We old hands remembered that it generally paid to plead ignorance in such a situation, since volunteering on the strength of some civilian achievement usually turned into a disaster.

"Anyone who has a piano at home, take two steps forward. Anyone who has a goldfish at home, step to the right. Anyone who's got a sister, step to the rear."

"Now then, the ones with a sister go to the kitchen for potato peeling. The piano players are to help the corporal to move the furniture. The ones with the goldfish are down for latrine cleaning." And so forth.

However, the situation was slightly different now. Surely nothing much could go wrong, and anyway there might be a chance to get improved living or working conditions. So step forward you coward; so I did, and with me a few more. The Old Man picked five of us and dismissed the rest. We were joined by the five civilians and told that, from now on, we all belonged to the transport section. Our Russian friends would drive the trucks on the night shift and we would have the day shift from 0800 to 1700 hours Eastern European time.

Coming as it did after a long period of being allowed only to do what one was told, when told to do it, this chance once more to exercise a certain amount of personal judgement came as quite a surprise. We chosen few walked over to the compound and were each adopted by one of the civilian drivers. They went to their vehicles, which all turned out to be Studebakers apart from an old SIS that seemed to have sprung from the days when Daimler was first designing cars. My opposite number was a tall, blond, blue-eyed tree-trunk of a man, by the name of Misha. He hailed from Siberia, he told me. As things turned out, I had been assigned to the funniest and most understanding driver of them all. He truly did have an immense sense of humour and a quick brain that not only matched his looks, but could focus on the matter in hand in an instant. I could not have had more luck.

He began to explain, "This machine needs some understanding. First and foremost, the compression of the engine is so high that you will not be strong enough to start it. It has to be crank started because the starter motor is faulty. Well, not so much faulty as there isn't one at all. In the morning I will get the engine going and you will have to keep it turning over all day long unless you can get a tow-start. For such emergencies I have my own tow line. You can't trust other drivers."

"Secondly the lorry has some other minor deficiencies. The gearbox has no synchromesh. You will have to time the gear changing to the revolutions of the engine, by ear naturally."

Fortunately I had some experience of a 'crash' gearbox already, because during my training for a driving certificate I had practised on a truck which had been liberated by the German Army from the French, and it had been as rudimentary as they come.

There was more to come.

"The first gear," he went on to explain, "will jump out of the cogs unless you hold it in position with both hands. You have to use both hands because, what with the vibration and the fact that the truck has a mind of its own, you will find that it constantly tries to get into second gear. You can't pull away in second gear, you understand, or the engine will stall. You then either wake me up so I can come out and swing the motor for you (fat chance) or you will have to get someone to give you a tow."

I tried frantically to understand and memorise every detail, but Misha was very patient. After allowing me time to adjust my thinking to the problem of handling his truck, he dropped a bombshell.

"As far as the steering lock is concerned, you can only turn the wheel a few degrees to the right. Don't worry. The left one will compensate for this. It means that when you try to get through the

gate of the compound you will have to steer in a large arc, otherwise
you will hit the fence. So what you do is... " at which point he began
drawing a diagram in the sand, sketching in the position of the camp,
the railway line, the road and the relative position of the crusher
compound.

"What you do is go on the left lock by the rail crossing, practically
heading towards that big oak tree over there," he said, pointing to it
with his drawing stick. "Then, when you are approximately in line
with the first tent of the army camp, pull hard to the right. This will
give you the direction to the centre of the gate. Once through, left
lock to bring you to the unloading place for the crusher. If you
continue from there, still on the left lock, you will make it through the
exit gate and out on the road back to Lopasaia. Got it? Don't worry,
we will practise."

He took a swig of water so he could continue, for obviously his
sermon was not at an end.

"One thing you must remember is that we have to save petrol so
we always have enough left over for our Sunday outings." No doubt I
would find out what that meant in due course. "In Russia the one who
works during the day and sleeps at night will starve. I do not intend
to go hungry. Got it?"

"One has to keep a logbook for the trips to and from the quarry.
The man in charge of the lorry park, our natschalnik, knows not only
the distance between the two points of call but also the petrol
consumption per kilometre for each lorry. In order to save petrol we
will have to let our vehicle roll down every gradient out of gear.
Once you have got the hang of driving the SIS, you will be able to
switch the engine off at the top of each hill and re-start it at the bottom
by engaging bottom gear. Remember, you need both hands to get into
gear."

"After your last run in the evening we will meet over there," and
he pointed in the direction of Lopasaia, "by that little wood and the
single tree, where we cannot be spotted from the park, and I will
siphon off the surplus petrol leaving only as much in the tank as there

should be. That's all. See you tomorrow; I will go with you a few times in the morning to make sure you do everything right. Dospidania (goodbye)."

Misha walked me back to the camp where my co-drivers felt sorry for me, having to team up on a dinosaur of a lorry, and at the time I found it hard to disagree with them. How wrong we all were. Events would show that I had actually drawn first prize.

Looking back over the forty-seven years since I first sat in that old SIS lorry, the events seem so very far away. It is almost as if everything happened in another century.

The feeling of freedom regained when I drove the first time to the quarry was indescribable. There I was, rolling along, all alone and without a guard, no worries and enjoying life. This could go on for ever. Along the new road I went, into town and gazing like a tourist on all the sights, taking in the sounds of the people as they shopped in the small street markets where they bought and sold garden produce. The only thing I had to concern me, really, was Misha's instruction to economise on petrol whenever I could.

The head of the quarry was a manager who operated with one of our work groups. Now and again they used dynamite to blast the stone, and this job was only ever handled by the Russian.

The first day passed without problems. I learnt to master my SIS and managed, at first assisted by my new friend Misha, to negotiate the turning into the compound and to avoid crashing into the gateposts. Misha was satisfied and so was I. That evening I drove to the rendezvous, where the contents of the petrol tank were adjusted down to the expected level, and I went back to camp to go through the motions of handing the vehicle over to Misha, now going on duty as the night driver.

After a couple of uneventful weeks we were all issued with special passes, similar to identity cards, which were designed to let us pass a road block set up over the weekend by the police outside Lopsaia. I asked Misha what it was all about, and he replied that this had to do with the expected arrival of a stream of peasants, who were being taken on foot from the Ukraine and the south to the eastern regions of the Soviet Union because an enormous drought had laid waste to that agricultural region. Apparently the sun had been shining relentlessly since April and, apart from a short burst of rain a week or so earlier, had seen no rainfall since the end of the winter. Now, everyone who could walk was being marched east – men, women and children – taking with them their one and only Party-permitted family cow, their buckets, spades and all.

As a result of this drought in the breadbasket of Russia, ordinary commodities like potatoes, watermelon and grain were in short supply, while meat was also hard to come by as well. Inflation was creeping in, and long queues formed in front of the shops.

Bread was virtually rationed. Out of a monthly average income of about two hundred and fifty roubles they had to spend fifty roubles just to buy a bucket of potatoes. However, on each side of the road to Lopsaia were large potato fields and because of what was going on in the food industry, those fields were guarded day and night by bailiffs armed with shotguns. But because there were many acres of potatoes and only a handful of shotgun bearers, the fields were not guarded very well.

Once the potato plants grew it seemed easier to keep control, for as long as there were no bare patches in the field everything was thought to be in good order. But never discount the ingenuity of the hungry. When the potatoes were ready for lifting, an eagle-eyed watcher would have been able to see shady figures crawling on their bellies far inside the fields to dig up the spuds. Having taken what they needed, they stuck the plant-tops back into the soil. For a couple of days after this the field looked all untouched, the bailiff was happy, and so were those who did the digging. But then the plants started to wilt and all over the potato acreage mysterious bare patches appeared, and when the experts went out to investigate the disease, everything was found out. But too late. As Misha had said, "Those who work during the day and sleep at night starve."

The first week of driving duty went along well, if one forgets the continual worry that the engine would stop with no hope of a tow in sight. Then Misha arranged to collect me on Saturday morning on the pretext that we had to repair our lorry; so that it would be fully operational on Monday, it was best that we use our weekend break for this. Very patriotic. So Misha came and off we went to the vehicle compound to do some fictitious work. Naturally, we had to take the lorry out for a test run and with much banging and grinding we left the site. A few kilometres south, Misha stopped. He turned to me with a wink and said, "We must help these poor peasants and ease their burden, don't you agree?"

Who was I to argue, for as the Good Book says, one should always try to help one's neighbour.

We drove a few more kilometres and waited by the roadside where there was a nice, gently sloping bank. Why Misha had selected this particular location soon became apparent, for down the road came lurching a peasant family, the old man in tatters, the woman (his wife?) in a dress which must have seen her or possibly many people through good times and bad over the past fifty years or so, and with them a cow, or what seemed to me to be the ghost of a cow. The poor creature was all hide and bones with her huge head dangling from a skinny neck. With each step she weaved from one side to the other and made a quite pathetic sight.

Misha approached the old man and opened negotiations. For what, I wondered. Were we not agreed that we would extend a helping hand? Misha explained later that this may be so, but there was a price for everything, even help, even human kindness! After some haggling, it was clear that a price had been agreed upon to transport man, woman, bucket, the couple's few belongings and cow as far as we could towards Lopsaia. One hundred roubles changed hands.

I had to back the lorry up to the bank, whereupon the cow was pushed on and tethered, and her owners squeezed into the driving cabin with us. Luckily, whoever designed that old SIS in the distant past had foreseen the need for a roomy cab.

Off we went, with me behind the wheel and Misha on the lookout for police militia. In those days anyone who wanted to carry anything but goods had to have a special permit, and the lorry was marked on the back accordingly. We certainly had no permit, and the lorry was not marked either. We drove around a bend, fortunately very slowly, and Misha spotted a road block and ordered me to stop. So far as our passengers were concerned we had come to the end of the journey. From here on the road to Lopsaia would be plastered with obstacles.

Out climbed the man and the woman and down came their few precious items. But what about the cow! It must have been the first time that she had had first-class treatment, riding on a lorry, and the experience must have frightened her to death. Consequently she had emptied whatever she had in her seven stomachs on to my beautiful vehicle. Only one expression came to mind. I have to say that I looked upon the poor creature and in disgust on the platform at the same time.

The question was how to get the cow off the truck. She had been tied up facing forward, but the exit was at the rear. There was no convenient embankment nor did we carry a ramp down which she could be coaxed.

"Get the rope," Misha commanded, "and tie it round the horns."

I climbed on to the roof of the cab, dutifully tied the rope around the cow's horns and, after being told to throw the rope to Misha, I climbed down to watch what he was going to do. Misha went over to a tree which happened to be right behind the lorry, slung the rope around and tied the end to the tow hook on the truck.

"Get in, Gans. Drive forward, slowly."

I must have looked startled, but he just smiled at me and said, "Don't you worry. As you drive forward the rope will pull the cow's head around and the rest of the cow will follow. She has no choice. She doesn't want to die, does she?"

Holding the gear lever with both hands in the first position and looking through the small rear window, I started to pull forward. Slowly, ever so slowly, the cow turned, and, when she had reached the end of the platform, duly jumped down. Her legs gave way for a moment, but she got up again smartly and looked as startled as the peasant, his wife and I did. Misha caught my eye and pointed first to his head and then to the formidable biceps of his left arm.

"You've got to have it here and not there, Gans."

Perfectly true, of course: think before using brute force.

This was the only time that we picked up passengers. There were none looking for a lift on weekends and we had no time during the week.

One day Misha wanted to come on my midday run. He did not tell me why until we reached the quarry, where he had a lengthy discussion with the plant manager. The end result was that money changed hands and the lorry was loaded with gravel instead of the usual rocks, and no entry was made in the logbook either.

"Go, Gans. I'll tell you where."

Misha guided me through the town and into a remote place on the outskirts until we stopped at a building site, where a small new house was being erected. Its new owner was waiting at the side of the road. In the blink of an eye, he and Misha unloaded the SIS, and Misha received a large bundle of bank notes for his service. He explained, "This friend of mine wants to build his house, but he cannot pay the asking price for the gravel that he needs for the foundation. So we just help him, ponial (got it)?"

Back we went to the quarry, this time loading the rock we were supposed to carry and carted it off to the crusher. The whole experience was most enlightening. It was another example of private enterprise which no one need know about. The petrol we used on the gravel run came out of our 'savings for unforeseen engagements', so that we would not run foul of our natschalnik's calculations.

It was now well into September. The new road had taken shape and was almost finished. Clearing up work had started and we could foresee the end of this assignment. By the end of September we learned that we would leave shortly for a new camp, Uzlovaya, south of Tula and about one hundred and fifty kilometres from Lopsaia. One morning, eight army lorries and a Jeep turned up and we bade farewell to the old oak tree and everything that went with it. I shook hands with Misha. We knew that we would never see each other again and when we pulled away and on to 'our' new road, I saw him standing there, forlornly waving his hand. Thank you, Misha, for a wonderful experience.

RACKETS PAVE THE WAY TO HELL

We reached Uzlovaya late that night to find the camp brightly illuminated in anticipation of our arrival. One transport had rolled in the day before and it was good to be able to greet our friends from Yavas, who had been working on another stretch of the road.

When the Russian camp administrators inspected the newcomers, I discovered that one of the team was our old, friendly political commissar captain, who had taken a shine to me at Yavas, with mixed feelings on my part. The large extended family of PoWs was almost complete, although we heard that the rest of our original contingent had been sent directly from Yavas to a coal mining camp further south where we would join them in due course. Nothing could have been worse than to be sent into the pits with no prior experience of mining.

For the time being, then, we were to stay in Uzlovaya. After a day of rest, parties were organised to work on harvesting cabbage, or on a building site, or to be available for special duties. By now the October freeze had begun and winter clothes were issued to us. I was to realise, later, how lucky I was to acquire a pair of long, baggy quilt trousers though at first I felt unhappy with them as they made me look like a circus clown.

My friend Hugo suggested that we should join the building team, remarking that it was pretty cold on the fields but with any luck we could look forward to having a roof over our head. There might even be comforting open fires to dry out the mortar and plaster. Hugo was right.

In modern terms this would have been a Do-It-Yourself paradise. We, the great untrained, were given the task of plastering interior walls. The rooms where we were to work were heated by open coal fires laid in remodelled petrol barrels. There was a slight snag: the plaster and mortar we were expected to spread had to be prepared in the bitter cold outside and was almost frozen by the time we received it, despite surrounding it with hot water. These were not the days of modern 'dry wall' plasterboard, but of applying the ancient form of lath and plaster by spreading the plaster directly and thickly on the walls.

Needless to say, because of the condition of the plaster when we got it, it did not stick properly on the walls and fell off in great chunks. After a few days, it was decided to abandon the attempt to build houses in the frost.

You might think that it was because we had become experts in working in cold buildings that we were next assigned to the local cold-storage warehouse for loading and stocking duties. Watched intently by the manager and his staff, we unloaded refrigerated railway wagons and delivered the goodies to their assigned chambers.

Apart from us, there was a party of Russian civilian workers who tried to divert some of the meat by letting the odd quarter of beef or lamb drop through the gap between the train and the platform. Now and again they were successful, and the 'liberated' food was skilfully caught by an accomplice hiding under the truck. We wondered if we might do the same, but the problem of how to get meat through the camp gate without being detected was too difficult to solve.

Things were different, however, when a load of small stuff arrived. Rabbits, ox tongues, liver etc., were much easier to handle, and our guards recognised this fact and carried out searches whenever we left the warehouse as well as when we arrived back in camp.

This is where my baggy trousers came into their own. I fastened a sturdy hook inside each trouser-leg and, when I just happened to let a tongue or a piece of liver slide into my trousers, I caught it on one of the two hooks. Of course it was no good taking just one piece of meat, as my trouser-legs had to balance to apply even weight to the waistband, in order to avoid having one trouser-leg longer than the other.

This worked like a charm and secured a supplementary food supply for us, the needy. But one day the warehouse manager discovered that a whole quarter of beef was missing and accused us of stealing it, so a thorough search was arranged. Of course, the missing beef would not be found as this was way outside our league. Nonetheless, when my turn came, I felt very apprehensive, knowing that, although no one could accuse me of grand larceny, I had the evidence of petty pilfering about my person. But the guard only searched the PoWs' pockets and touched the outside of their trousers, so my two tongues made their way safely into the camp kitchen.

We certainly had a variety of work. One day we were switched from meat to the grain store, where the main item being stored was buckwheat. Once again my baggy trousers came into their own. By tying them tightly at the ankles I turned them into two sacks below the knees. Walking became difficult, and it took some practice to be able to cover the ground without rolling like a drunken sailor or stumbling along like an old man. My comrades came to my aid whenever we went back to camp, letting me walk in the middle and thus concealing my very uncertain gait.

These days of plenty were fated not to last very long, and just before Christmas our duties were again switched. This time we found ourselves at the site of a newly sunk coal pit where we were to assist in the construction of concrete water towers.

As group leader, I had to complete daily report forms every evening and, fortunately, by this time I had become quite good at writing in Russian. This fact, I was soon to discover, had been appreciated by the camp administrators who had a major problem on their hands. Here was a new coal pit, with hundreds of men and women working hard on day and night shifts, but there was nobody available to pay their wages. The reason was that the wages officer had been taken ill, and there was no civilian replacement to be found. I was 'volunteered' for the job. It was challenging work, involving the calculation of earnings of the various grades of male and female workers. The chance to work in an office appealed to me and I accepted.

Recognising that this was not my everyday run-of-the-mill work, the mine managers arranged for me to have a short introductory course in Soviet wages policy. It would have been really difficult without it.

Actually, the job was quite fascinating. It introduced me to the intriguing ways in which Mr and Mrs Average Citizen had their wages determined. Bottom of the pile came everyone who either could not or did not work to a 'Standard', and they received a basic wage of two hundred and fifty roubles a month. Higher ranked employees got a bit more, but not much.

Many of the Russians were on a form of piece work, their income being related to the degree to which they met individual targets. They got a flat rate accorded to the standard output in their class of work, but if they fell short of the target their wage was reduced by the percentage of the shortfall. Equally, if they exceeded their target, they received that percentage more than the flat rate.

So far so good. However, whichever way one looked at individual weekly income, it was not enough. Understandably, perhaps, the system allowed for a fair bit of corruption. There was a saying in those days that the good worker got his percentage written, the bad one had to work for it. This meant that the one who was well in with his superior would have one hundred per cent plus entered into his daily performance record, whereas the worker who fell from grace, or was simply not well liked, had percentages deducted from his record, offsetting the extra given to the 'good workers'. The trick was that by agreement with the manager, the one who profited from the racket split the excess earnings equally with him (the manager). By this means everybody gained, with the exception of the 'bad' guy, who was the one hundred per cent loser.

It could also happen that the standard target was such that nobody, no matter how hard they worked, could meet it. In this case, by agreement, one or two of the gang were allotted high percentages and their 'surplus' was then divided between the consenting parties. Instead of receiving nothing at all, by this means everyone got at least something. The racket was worked where standing charges were being deducted automatically from earnings, such as rent etc., in which case the 'non-earners' would have been left with so little money that they would be bound to live below the poverty line.

There could be another type of situation, as for example arises where the standard norm, or target, made no allowance for changes in working conditions. A good example would be the handling of different types of soil. Soil came in six categories: sand, firm sand, soil, clay, gravel and rock.

Bureaucracy had decided that because sand is light and easy to excavate, a worker could fully meet the norm of two cubic metres per day, both in summer and winter. However, the fact was that, particularly in Russia, the soil froze in the winter, making it quite impossible to dig out as much sand then as in the summer. In these circumstances the 'good guys' were protected by a most devious method. First ascertain how much had been excavated in total, allocate a high percentage to one or two people, and make sure that the overall total did not exceed the day's work achievement.

To aggravate my wage list I also had to remember one of the cardinal rules of Communism: 'Those who do not work need not eat.' Never mind whether one had fallen ill, or had suffered a work injury; if they had to stay away from work until they were fit again, then they were not entitled to any pay.

What was I to do? I had the old-fashioned idea that man had to eat or he would die. It is quite incredible for me to recall that, during my PoW days as wages manager, I had to subjugate my own feelings absolutely and play a part in administering a system that was riddled with social chicanery. What can have been the feelings of these poor creatures, on the verge of starvation, when they felt obliged to come to me, a foreigner and a PoW to boot, to beg for a cash advance so they could buy something to eat?

This was the sort of thought process I had to go through: last week you actually earned eight-four roubles, so fifty per cent of that can be given now as an advance, but half of that will have to be repaid from the next weekly payout; if you don't earn enough next week to cover the repayment, bad luck – you ask for another advance of fifty per cent of the outstanding money, to be repaid next week in addition to what is still outstanding; however, if the total debt exceeds two weeks' estimated pay, I can give you nothing.

I had women in tears in my office on payday, begging me to help them, but I could do nothing. It was literally more than my life was worth, though not being part of the system had the advantage that everyone eventually came to recognise that I was not open to corruption or persuasion, and did everything by the book. I was obliged to ignore what I am sure may have been quite true statements – that the old wages clerk always helped them by advancing more in return for a monetary token of 'appreciation'.

But strictness was something they understood, as had their forebears since the days of the Tsars. Once they realised that nobody could be at an unfair financial advantage so long as I had the job, they accepted both their position and me.

Those weeks as a civilian wages clerk opened my eyes to one aspect, at least, of the way in which the working Russian population was treated by those in authority, and shone a light on the very open and generally recognised inequalities which made it possible for some people to lead a privileged life, benefiting from the toil of others without really doing anything to warrant such rewards.

My job came to an end when it was decided to dissolve the Uzlovaya Camp and I moved with the rest of the prisoners to join our advanced party in Lager 388/8 Stalinogorsk (as it was known then), our first 'coal pit' camp, lying south of Tula. By lorry, again, the trip took about six hours. Once again we arrived at night, to find the pit and the camp bathed in floodlight; the camp, because it awaited our convoy, the pit because it worked three shifts around the clock. The sight of the pit highlighted against the night sky drove a shudder down my spine. The wheels on the winding tower revolved and their spokes, counter-rotating in the glare of a floodlight, produced a surreal pattern which turned the entire scene into a nightmare.

WE WERE AN UNGRATEFUL BUNCH

Lager 388/8 was on all counts a very spacious camp, covering an area greater than any of those I had encountered before, apart from the one in Romania. Prisoners were housed in four barracks, each accommodating about four hundred men. The one in which I ended up also contained the tailor's workshop and the hairdresser's den. Each barrack hut had two enormous brick-built stoves, so sited that between them they would heat the entire length of the long building, and these were kept burning day and night. They were tended by men in Category Four because they were unable to work at all. By the entrance, which was on one of the long sides, was a drying chamber for our wet pit outfits.

Each of us had his own bunk-bed, a straw mattress covered with a bed cloth, a straw-filled pillow case and two blankets. Some of us could not bear eating in the dining hall and took our food back to our bunks to eat. Strange though it may seem, although the bunk was one of hundreds in a single huge shed, it took on the feel of a walled-off private space. The walls were invisible, of course, but everyone respected the privacy of 'bed spaces' so religiously that the walls might just as well have been made of brick.

The camp hospital had been set up by the main gate, close to the administration block which housed the camp commandant, a Major Sub, and his helpers. The remaining buildings were used as bathhouse and delousing station, workshops, clothing store and kitchen/dining block. The dining hall doubled as the camp theatre with stage, dressing rooms and a musicians' rehearsal room. There was no library, although there was a very small collection of books in the hospital.

As originally planned, there was nowhere for the invariable Anti-Fascist, so he had to make do with a small compartment on his own. Albert, as I seem to remember him being called, became a big shot in East Germany after his return.

One important break with routine, so far as this camp was concerned, was that we were never counted as a whole. The only head counts were taken whenever we left camp for the pit.

The day after our arrival we able-bodied men were given medical exams, then classified and divided into three working shifts. The shifts ran from 8:00 a.m. to 4:00 p.m., 4:00 p.m. to midnight, and midnight to 8:00 a.m. Wilfried, Heinz and I were assigned to the night shift for the time being.

The rest of the day stretched out before us, leaving dreadful hours of hanging about before we were to go down a mine for the first time in our lives. None of us had any idea what lay in store. I wondered if I would be overcome by claustrophobia underground. How would I react to the whole environment?

We had a foreboding at the midday meal when it was pointed out that we would now have an increased daily ration of bread, from 600g to 900g, as we would be working below ground.

The night was dark and frosty and, despite the fact that I was wearing a warm quilted jacket ('bouphica' in Russian), I shivered because under it I had on only flimsy pit clothes. The coldest part of me, though, was my feet. The issue of special footwear consisted of rubber shoes on to which fibrous extensions had been sewn so that they reached halfway up the calves. Rubber is a good conductor of heat and cold, so it was hardly surprising that my feet soon seemed as cold as the ground beneath.

In fact, the only way to keep the blood circulating was to dance a jig: on to the left foot, on to the right foot, one foot forward and one foot back. It was unreal to see the entire night shift jumping up and down, and stepping to the left or the right, totally unsynchronised.

The head count completed, I found myself walking towards the dark silhouettes of the mine buildings. It was only about two hundred metres from the camp to the mine, but so sick was I with apprehension that it seemed much further.

We assembled in the general assembly hall of the main building and were given our first instructions. The older hands already had their jobs and knew how to go about mining, or transporting coal, or developing new galleries. The mine being comparatively new, there was not much actual coal production, as the main gallery and its side tunnels were still being developed. We, the newcomers, were attached to the transport section.

Because the mine was still small, with the longest run of rails no more than four hundred metres, no locomotives were yet available to move the small trucks, so we would have to move everything by hand. Two bodies per truck was the norm. Each of us was given a miner's lamp, not for the light it gave so much as to monitor the existence of methane gas.

"As soon as the little flame begins to die down, retreat quickly and with caution," we were told. "And remember to cause no sparks, or you might blow yourself up."

Nice prospect. Finally we were told to whom to report, and where to assemble once we reached the bottom of the shaft. Off we went, up the steps to the loading platform of the winding tower.

The apron of the lift platform was dimly lit by only a few forlorn light bulbs, which transformed the place into a set for Wagner's Dawn of the Gods. It was unreal and eerie. The lift cages arrived in quick succession and spat out their loads of humans, coal or waste, the first quickly stepping out into the cool night and hurrying down the steps as if wanting to escape the black hole which had kept them for eight hours, the latter in iron trucks, being pulled away and pushed out into the darkness to be disposed of on the slag heap where the coal was separated as much as possible from the clay and sand.

Among those ahead of us waiting to go down were a few Russian miners, mostly occupied on underground mechanical and electrical maintenance, for the mine was actually only being worked by PoWs, under the watchful eyes of two or three Russian mining engineers. I must admit that I shuddered with trepidation at being lowered into the bowels of the earth and was quite glad when the call for boarding was delayed as the area below had first to be cleared of trucks. But inevitably the moment came when I was squashed into one of the cages between my fellow countrymen. Everyone's heart was beating like a steam hammer. I repeatedly told myself that things couldn't be all that bad and that I would get used to this ordeal.

What I did not then, and certainly would not have considered even likely, was that everyone who works at a coal face eventually becomes addicted to coal – to eating, sleeping, talking coal and nothing but coal, coal, coal. In time I would actually come to understand why generations of miners keep on in the trade.

On disembarking from the cage at the foot of the shaft, we assembled in a side tunnel which also housed the generator. All electricity in the mine was Direct Current, and the bulbs lit from it gave to the whole place a cold and uninviting appearance. DC light bulbs emit a cold, soft light, especially when they are powered by only twelve volts. The generator hummed insistently; compressed air for the pneumatic hammer drills leaked away with a gentle hiss; rolling trucks rumbled in the semi-darkness and the command bell used to signal the lift operator clanged at intervals. All these sounds served to make the whole scene even more sinister.

When my partner and I were called to follow the gang working at the face of the main tunnel, I had an attack of nerves. The tunnel at that point was in almost complete darkness, picked out here and there by the dim light of our miners' lamps. One after the other we walked along the narrow gauge railway line, water running down the walls and raining from the ceiling. The clay underfoot was not only liquid mud, but formed large puddles where the ground dipped. I managed to step into one of these puddles without warning, splashing the grey ooze all over me. I was wet through after only a few steps into hell.

There was another problem in walking down the tunnel, in that I kept hitting my head against a ceiling beam or a side pillar because I was walking as I did above ground instead of being stooped, while my eyes were not looking the right way. How on earth can one look straight ahead to avoid bumping into anything that should not be there, while at the same time scanning the ceiling for unwanted protrusions and at the same time looking to the left or right to avoid the timber along the side walls? You learn the art of mine walking very quickly once you get a few nasty knocks on the head and the shoulder and sink into a muddy, stinking puddle which one could have avoided.

The way to walk through a mine, I soon discovered, was to walk like a hunchback, with one hand on the back, with the other hand holding the miner's lamp and dangling down at your side. The stance is very much like that of an orang-utan on the prowl, but it does enable one to illuminate the path immediately in front, as well as the ceiling right above and the nearside wall, by constantly moving the lamp in an elliptical pattern, swivelling the head down, to the side, up and back again. If one does all that in a co-ordinated manner, one can cover the ground remarkably quickly and avoid the hidden dangers without stumbling. A cross-eyed person must do quite well underground, I guess.

The party we had to serve was engaged in driving the main tunnel forward and opening up the coal seams. This is probably a good time for me to explain how a mine is laid out, as it will make it easier to follow my story.

Imagine a double-sided comb. The spine is the main tunnel and the headings are the teeth to the left and right of it. Now break off every tenth tooth, making a gap between blocks of teeth. Each block represents one coal seam and the gap is the roadway which takes the conveyor belt.

At the end of this roadway, to the left or right, one drives a channel, about two metres wide, into the block of coal and thereby opens up the first working. Along this a chain conveyor is installed. As you chip out the coal, working towards the main tunnel for a depth of about four metres, it is shovelled on to the chain conveyor, which in turn spits it out on to the main conveyor running down the main tunnel and transports it to the end where it is loaded into trucks. During the extraction operation the parts of the seam which have been excavated are supported, in our case using timber.

This happens on each side of the transport tunnel and so forth until the entire block has been hauled out.

The seams in this mine were comparatively high, about two and a half metres, overlying clay. There was sand above, which made working quite dangerous, for sand above, we were told, is worse than water. If the ceiling were to collapse the sand would come thundering down, destroying everything in its path and leaving behind a cave large enough for a three-bedroomed bungalow.

On that first day, our task as transport people was to push the little wagons, each holding about one ton of coal or waste. We pushed them all the way up the main tunnel to the lift, collected an empty truck, pushed it all the way back, turned around and started the whole procedure again. This was no small task, particularly as the roadway was by no means level for all its length. But we soon learnt how to make good use of the downhill gradient to get up the next hill without too much effort.

In between trips we had to wait until our truck had been loaded again. During this welcome pause, I would always sit down and rest, sometimes dozing off. Prolonged interruptions came when the compressed air supply failed and the pneumatic hammer drills had to rest and I made the utmost of these occasions. Throughout my time in captivity, my number one priority was always to take the weight off my feet whenever and wherever I could, in order to preserve vital calories and strength. Fortunately I had the gift of being able to sleep anywhere and at any time. This had been true even during the course of the War.

The first day passed without incident, but we had a lot of hard, and at times unnecessary, work. Wilfried and I timed the last delivery so that we would not leave surplus material behind, but made it to the lift when the new shift arrived, hoping to be able to get home early. We still had a lot to learn. After waiting for a while we were able to take a lift which was only half-full, but when we arrived at the top the sentry made us wait around until he had collected a large enough bunch of PoWs to take to the Pit Admin Block, so that he would not have to climb the steep steps to the ground floor level too often. He wore a sheepskin coat and warm felt boots. We, on the other hand, had only our flimsy, soaking wet pit dress. The temperature at the top was eight degrees below freezing and in next to no time our clothes were frozen stiff as boards. When we were allowed to leave, every step we took creaked like rusted door hinges as the ice cracked in the joints of our trousers.

Next time around we stayed down below as long as we could!

The assembly room in the administration building was not heated, but warm enough to thaw our clothes, which was not much help as they froze again as we made our way to the camp. Once we got back to our huts there were helping hands to peel off our garments and transfer them to the drying room. A short wash in the bathhouse and fresh underwear restored our faith in life. Off to the kitchen next, to receive our daily morning rations, and then to bed for a good rest. Not that we were able to get one. The constant traffic to the tailor's den at the far end of the hut and to the barber's, plus the noise made by the returning day shift and the departing afternoon shift, were not really conducive to sleep. Dozing rather than sleeping did not help much to restore lost energy, and I for one was usually out and about by early afternoon.

This sort of life went on for the next three years and it is surprising that I survived in one piece.

As day followed day I carefully watched the fellow cutting the coal with his pneumatic hammer and learned how to 'read' the coal. This meant that I was able to judge the way it was formed and what to watch out for, in order to determine how much was left before getting back into the sand, of which there were about thirty metres above us. I was fascinated by the way the coal fell almost effortlessly from the wall, and remembered the lessons I had learned in those far-off days on road making when we had to split granite rocks. Everyone handled coal in much the same manner, knowing where to apply the force so that the rest would come down automatically.

After a few weeks we learned that there was an opening for a coal face worker, so I applied for the job, put a crew together and immediately found my life not only changed for the better, but was so challenging that my working periods became quite exciting.

Back in camp everything continued as normal. The only difference was that those of us who had been officers suddenly began to receive a kilogram of sugar each month, as well as a few hundred grams of butter or margarine and a ration of real tobacco. Meat was available to the kitchen so that the officer caste might have special food, but we refused to be treated differently from the rest and insisted that the meat be used for the general cooking. The sugar and the butter we divided among our closest friends.

Every month there was a shift change, as a result of which the first shift became the third, the third the afternoon shift and the second shift the first.

The worst shift to be on was the third one, owing to the fact that one's rest period came during the noisiest and most disturbing time of the day. It was almost impossible to get into bed before about eleven o'clock, after washing and eating, only to be woken by the returning morning shift a few hours later, followed by the call for the second meal. There was not much chance of sleep after that, either. Then at 10 p.m. it was time to get up and fetch the third meal of the day and prepare for setting off for the pit at 11.30. It is hard to conceive, looking back, how much we looked forward to being on the day shift, though even this had its own drawbacks.

For instance, it was the day shift that turned out to unload timber trains as soon as they arrived, on the basis that the 'day' men had the longest rest during the night.

And, speaking of rest, there was never a Sunday day off in this camp.

Once each month we had the mixed pleasure of undergoing a medical examination. It was a mixed pleasure because, provided we played our cards properly, it could be turned to our own advantage. The administration's reason for the exam was to make sure that people were correctly assigned to the three work categories and the fourth, for which any work was too strenuous.

Put nakedly, if we were strong enough to go on working full weeks at the coal face we were, in effect, deemed to be so fit that we did not need much time off. However, from time to time most of us – and I, most certainly – felt in need of a bit of a rest. The only way of achieving this was to be medically down-graded for a spell.

The trick in such circumstances was to weigh as little as possible and hope that the records would show a loss of weight, no matter how small. A couple of pounds could make all the difference between being classified as fit for Category One, or only suitable for Categories Two or Three. I was personally against ending up in Category Four if this could be avoided, as that would mean one were suffering from almost total malnutrition. From such a state it was very hard to be upgraded to be fit enough to return to work.

In the normal course of events, work was important to me – not to say vital – as it took my mind off the awful fact of being shut away from home and family for an eternity.

If one decided to play the weight game, then, it was best to take the medical immediately after coming off shift; also it was essential to visit the latrine for physical enlightenment. I remember anxiously watching the pointer on the scales swing round to 56kg. The doctor seemed worried by this and flipped through the pages of his manual before certifying me as fit for Category Three. This meant that until further notice, and subject to there being no improvement in my medical condition, I would be restricted to working on Monday, Wednesday and Friday. But on four days of the week I would only receive 600g of bread – as though resting alone would improve my condition and make the scales jump for joy.

The medical examination was conducted with a charming lack of sophistication. For instance, after we were weighed the doctor pressed the shin, to see if there was any water under the skin, and pinched the bottom, to see whether there was still enough flesh to bother about.

Anyway, on the day in question when I was downgraded, I realised that something clearly had to be done to at least get some cash so I could acquire enough food to supplement the camp diet. As my former civilian friend, Misha, put it, "Those who work during the day and sleep at night starve."

I immediately began to scheme.

Come the autumn of 1947, we were informed that from then on we would receive the same wages as everybody else working in the mines, and for our general information the wage scales were posted on the notice board. These showed that the first 265 roubles we earned would be retained to cover the costs of our keep, the next 250 roubles would be paid to the individual worker and the rest would be banked in his name for the future. This meant, of course, that anyone who was not earning more than 265 roubles would get nothing for himself.

At this point I was reminded of our old friend 'the norm' and how when I was in charge of handing out wages I had learned that 'good workers get their earnings guaranteed, bad ones have to work for them'. Now it was our turn to set up our own money-earning racket. This was comparatively easy as all team leaders had to submit their own records. Those involved in the scheme were told how much of their norm had not been achieved or the extent to which they had exceeded it, and that the over-achievers would divide their 'written' earnings among the group so that everyone would at least receive some money with which to buy any extra food that might become available in the state shop outside the camp.

Our Russian colleagues were extremely helpful and gladly undertook to obtain the goods for us. It cannot have been easy for them, particularly when their own rations were exhausted and they emerged from the bakery shop with an armful of bread for us. We were never let down by any of them. When one of our own high earners had a surfeit of food, and this did happen from time to time, he made sure that his helper received a princely reward.

Wages were graded for the type of work being performed, so it was possible for men with the most dangerous tasks, such as seeing to the controlled caving-in of spent workings, to earn as much as two thousand roubles a month. Average income for a worker at the coal face was in the region of seven hundred and fifty roubles, transport workers got three hundred and fifty to four hundred roubles and the district manager earned nine hundred roubles.

One day, when my picking at the coal was interrupted by a power cut, I took up a piece of clay and started modelling, only to find that for this purpose it was good raw material. I took a piece back to the camp not really knowing what to do with it. Later, when I was passing the kitchen I saw our head of the cookery department smoking a pipe. The following day was one of my rest days and I sat at the table and made a clay pipe.

A very nice and elegant smoking implement it turned out to be, some twenty-five centimetres long, slightly curved and with a carved head. I set it in the drying room for two days and the following night, when I had the fire watch, laid it on a piece of wire mesh on top of the red hot cinders of the dying oven fire.

In the morning I retrieved a perfectly fired clay pipe, which was admired by all and sundry. I must admit that I was very proud of this creation, and I managed to persuade one of my friends, who was working in the joinery section, to make me a small case for it so it would not get shattered. I had not been to all this trouble for myself, you understand, the main object of the exercise being to use it for trade. The next, major, step was to approach the chief of the kitchen to try to arrange a sale and I had the great joy of striking success first time. He was delighted. His eyes glowed in anticipation of smoking his first clay pipe and parading it proudly in front of his colleagues. Naturally we haggled a bit over the price, but in the end settled on seven days' double rations of soup and kasha.

My first sale over, I was encouraged to make more pipes and sell them to whoever could afford the going rate of a piece of bread.

The following days and nights of my rest days were devoted to pipe manufacturing. In the process I discovered that their colour varied from batch to batch, some being grey, some marbled or rusty-red with a slight tinge of yellow. It seemed that this stemmed from the various ores of iron, sulphur or fool's gold contained in the clay. Once I had appreciated this, my business flourished as I was able to make pipes to order. It was not mass production, of course, and it took the best part of a week to make one that I thought was good enough to sell, but every week I managed to deliver one to another delighted customer. For the improved, custom-made, model I raised the price to 300g of bread per day for seven days.

The trouble was that there were not enough eligible pipe smokers and I could see that my food supply would dry up in due course unless I put on my thinking cap and came up with a fresh idea. I really struck lucky this time. Strolling through the camp I found out that all the huts' electrical wiring was to be renewed. This was a typical low-cost contract job, with all the actual wire runs carried out on the surface, supported by porcelain insulators. Those insulators must cost the administration a fortune, I thought. Why couldn't I produce them? If I were able to save the camp managers lots of lovely roubles, this poor undernourished Category Three prisoner might restore his weight and get back to working a full week.

The solution lay in using pit clay, so next time I was underground I made sure that a fair portion of the clay found its way into camp. Actual production of the insulators proved to be easy. I took a board, a twelve centimetre nail and a piece of thin wire, then kneaded the clay and formed it into a sausage approximately one and a half centimetres thick. Then I cut it into regular sections using the length of wire as though I were cutting cheese in a delicatessen. Each piece was three centimetres long. These I laid on the board and rolled them across the nail one centimetre from one end, thus making a groove and producing a collar. I stood each sausage upright and pierced a hole down the middle. The end result was a perfectly adequate, unfired insulator.

On my first experimental production run I made about ten of them and, using the experience with clay pipes, dried them slowly first and then fired them in the hot embers. The most beautiful insulators emerged from the ashes.

I went to see our camp commandant, Major Sub, and explained to him that we, the destroyers of the motherland, should do something to help the administration save money, and opened my fist for him to see my sample insulator. It was as though every molecule of his brain began to work overtime. I could see him thinking how all the money which had been allocated by the authorities for the rewiring job could be put to several other purposes, like a new dress for Mrs Sub!

"How many can you make?" he asked.

"About fifty a week," I replied. "I know that may not sound many, but, because of the consistency of the raw material, fifty percent will be destroyed in the firing as undetectable ores in the clay stay damp and explode in the oven when the moisture turns to steam."

He took the bait and the proffered explanation, so I continued, "There is one more thing, Major. Presently I am Category Three and, remembering your words that, 'each shovel of coal is a grenade for peace', I would like to get back to full employment as soon as possible and throw my whole weight back into the peace process. Would you please authorise for the period of my involvement in producing insulators double rations of soup and kasha, please sir?"

He smiled and told me to report to him each Friday and deliver my goods, whereupon I would receive written authorisation for a further seven days' of improved rations.

Smile, Gans, smile, I thought. You've pulled it off. Wilfried and Heinz will be pleased.

After obtaining sufficient supplies of clay, the next couple of days were devoted to the manufacture of insulators. I made hundreds of them, sufficient for the rewiring operation. After they were fired, I stored them under my bunk in a lockable box. Every Friday I took out the fifty I had promised and delivered them to Major Sub who duly handed over a chit allowing me to get my double rations. After the initial effort and overtime work I never made another insulator again. Thankfully Sub never found out!

Slowly I regained my weight, but in the process began to lose my hair. All over my head I developed round bald patches about the size of the old British half crown coin. I was shattered and went to the hospital where the doctor, again a woman, was perplexed and had no answer. Were they caused by lice? We had none, and anyway lice didn't eat hair. She was quite concerned about my condition and, no doubt to cover herself in case there was an outbreak of whatever I had, she decided to take me into hospital for observation.

What luxury. White linen, proper beds, lots to read, chess and people to play with – I felt truly pampered. A medical commission arrived and I was shown off to it as the curiosity of Lager 7388, a true specimen for unresolved medical research into the cause of circular hair loss. Wrinkled foreheads, murmured opinions and a verdict. It was decided there was nothing to worry about, and the hair loss would not be permanent. The trouble, they determined, was a vitamin deficiency, so I was prescribed plenty of Vitamin A. The next day I found myself released from hospital armed with a large glass full of the vital Vitamin A, three tablets to be taken after meals.

I began to worry. The insulator business would come to an end sooner or later and I had become used to having decent portions of sauerkraut soup and kasha. What else could I think of?

One day I went to the kitchen later than usual and was attracted by music and oratory coming from the room behind the stage. Being naturally inquisitive, I peered round the corner and found myself in the middle of some rehearsal. I watched for a while and asked if there was any chance of an opening in the concert party for someone who was good at composing funny poems and was also, by his own assessment, an acceptable compere. I recited one of my recent 'works' which described certain episodes of camp life and must have impressed the 'director' of the band of budding actors, for he immediately offered me a place. This was just the thing to occupy my brain and keep my thoughts away from the everlasting concern of being a PoW.

The concert party was a pillar of Lager life and greatly supported by the Russian authorities, who granted certain privileges to its members. You could grow your hair – if you had any to grow – and were allowed to wear civilian clothes made by the camp tailors. We were also provided with clean shirts and underwear at any time and, most important of all, received additional rations from the kitchen. I had joined the Lager hierarchy.

There was another, quite different, privilege. Each member of the concert party was also issued with a special pass, a 'propusk', which permitted one to leave the camp at will, and to go on an outing on Sundays to Stalinogorsk, the nearest town, without a guard. Usually one or two Russian soldiers came with us, more for fun than because they were worried that we might run away. With such privileges, who would?

Rehearsals were every afternoon. Cabaret, sketches, musicals and anything that would provide some entertainment to the general Lager public and Russians alike.

My first stage appearance was reading my own 'Glimpses of Lager Life' – sneering and humorous remarks about what had happened during a fortnight in and around the camp in chapter and verse, so to speak. After only a few performances, where I read my high quality poetry, my fellow inmates were actually looking forward to the next instalments. But soon my acting became more serious, as I was cast more and more often in female roles. Suitably made-up and put into pretty dresses and short skirts, not to forget high-heeled shoes, it seems that I became a rather delectable creature. But those high heels were torture!

Our theatrical performances won the acclaim of our Russian administration and it was decided to send us to entertain other camps. As our own shows were once every fortnight, the weekends between were available for such ventures. A theatre lorry was equipped with all our props, costumes, backdrops etc., and off we went on our tour around the country. I must admit that these were great times, full of excitement, as one could leave the confinement of our own camp and the rigours of the coal pit, and indulge in conversations with fellow sufferers about our common experiences.

The downside was that I put on weight and was upgraded once again to Category Two, which meant going down the pit full-time on dreaded shift work. However, I had not appreciated how persuasive was the theatre group, which negotiated with the management that, in order to keep the crowd smiling, I would only have to work the day shift on weekdays. The Russians agreed that we served a vital purpose in the Russian Five Year Plan.

In all honesty, I was not very keen to be going down the hole again and, with a bit of good old string-pulling, managed to transfer to the above ground saw-mill. Being reduced to 600g of bread and cut down to a basic income of three hundred and twenty-five roubles a month was no big sacrifice. The loss of a few calories was made up for by the additional rations to which we were entitled because of our noble cause and the loss of some of our free time.

Life was relatively rosy, but it would have been much more bearable if only we could hear now and again from home. Months passed with the only news we could get of the outside world coming by way of our Russian co-workers. What we did learn from them was that in the Soviet Union food was scarce, accommodation was rare and wages were low. We learned of strikes in the coal fields of Siberia and the deportation of thousands of citizens. Understandably, we were concerned about the rumours of a food shortage and wondered if that might mean us having to tighten our own belts. Fortunately it never came to that.

The whole nation was rocked at the end of 1947 by the impact of currency reform. The rouble was devalued overnight without any warning with the result that, for ten roubles the night before, there was now effectively just one. Our own savings accounts were also devalued. Wages did not rise in line with this devaluation so the real sufferers, of course, were the ordinary Russian citizens. Out of an average income of two hundred and fifty roubles they had to pay ten roubles for a two kilo loaf of bread and fifty roubles for a bucket of potatoes. Fish and meat were scarce but affordable in the state-run shops, sugar and butter were available only occasionally and vegetables could only be bought on the open market.

We prisoners were not affected by the general food shortages, though. Our rations may have been barely sufficient to sustain us underground workers, but they kept us in reasonable condition. We were certainly healthy enough to withstand the onslaught of rain in the pit, and cold above during the winter months. I cannot recall that any of us caught pneumonia or even had a bad cold. Human beings can be extraordinarily tough. All that one had to do was to conserve as much energy as possible – sit, sleep and daydream of better times to come. All this would end one day. Nothing is for ever. Never mind, 'scoro budit'.

One day I was approached by the Russian pit manager, who knew me from the time of my rescue from a deluge of sand and my tunnelling operations, and asked if I would be interested in going underground again. I would not be on a working crew, but instruct young Russian miners. They, after all, were the ones who would have to take over the working of the pit in due course.

I was not quite sure what to say. Was I honoured to have been chosen for such an unusual request? I explained about my involvement in the theatre group and that I wanted to work during the day only.

"That's no problem. Instruction is restricted to the first shift, anyway."

"Pay?" I asked.

"Statutory and as per regulations. Seven hundred and fifty roubles per month."

We had a deal!

The message was passed on to the camp administration, and from the following Monday I found myself in charge of four Russian would-be miners. As usual with newcomers, they knew it all. They had read thick books about mining and what to do and when and how. It was quite clear that they took the gravest exception at having to listen to this German upstart and follow his instructions.

The first few days were not very amusing and called for a lot of patience and persuasion to make them pay attention. I wondered if we would all get along a lot better if I were to give them a relatively free hand, so I put a pneumatic hammer into their hands and let them loose on the coal. After all, that was what they wanted to do.

Remembering my granite block days, I sat back and allowed them to rattle their biceps to bits. As I fully expected, not much coal came off that face and my young hopefuls made little progress, driving the shaft forward only one metre.

I confronted them with their abysmal results and told them that their income would be a minus quantity if they carried on like that. Would they please listen to me and watch whilst I worked the hammer and did the explaining. They got the message, all right. Happily for all of us, when the mine director came to see how his protégés were progressing, I was able to tell him that they would one day be 'Stachanovski Activists'.

How his face glowed, and theirs as well. Stachanov was a Russian miner, who, some years ago and in honour of one Red Remembrance Day, had decided that he would work like mad and break all known coal haulage records. He did, producing one hundred and sixty-four tons in one shift. Whether he did it entirely on his own or was aided and abetted was never recorded. He got himself hauled in front of Papa Stalin who pinned on his breast the gold star of the 'Hero of Socialist Workers', or some such.

Stachanov's example was the leitmotif of all truly convinced Red Workers. Whoever performed better and did considerably more than the norm had asked for became a 'Stachanovski Activist', whether they were male or female.

I remember one exceptional case, which was spread all over the front pages of the Soviet press, where a stable maid on a pig farm, who nursed a sow, got the gold star for helping to deliver twelve piglets, all dropped by the same animal. We christened her 'The Norm Accomplishing Mother Sow'.

At the beginning of 1948 the pit was ready for full production. By this time we had prepared three districts, taken delivery of locomotives and psyched up the mine administration to look to a bumper coal harvest. After all, all the coal seams were high and close to the lift, so transport was no problem. More Russian miners arrived, to be taught by my former students.

At this point I was taken off teaching and promoted to district manager. This meant that I did not have to work physically any more, but had to go into the mine once in every shift to see that everything was in good order. Mostly I stayed nearly one full shift, at my choice, within my own district. Whenever possible I opted for the day shift, for obvious reasons.

Returning to the surface one day, my two colleagues and I were summoned to Major Sub and, with a certain amount of trepidation, asked our camp interpreter to accompany us. That turned out to be a good idea.

"Now listen," said the Major, looking sternly at us but seeming to direct himself mainly at me. He probably thought, after the insulator affair, that I might be the best target to address.

"I want to know why you lot are ungrateful."

We looked startled and did not know what to make out of that peculiar question.

"Just answer me a few questions. Do you have a roof over your head?" We nodded in agreement. "See here, not all of my people outside have their own roof over their heads. Do you have your own bedstead, with a mattress, a linen pillow case, blankets with linen covers? I know the bed is filled with straw and so are the pillow cases. But all of you have all that for yourself. Right?" '

Again we nodded.

"See, my people outside do not have all that either. Many have to sleep on bare floors, eight, ten to one room. Do you receive three times per day a warm meal? Oh, I know it's only cabbage soup with not much in it, and kasha?"

"Yes," we said.

"See, my people outside have not got that every day, as you have. Sometimes they have to go without because the provisions have run out or are not available at all. You get bread every day, don't you? I know, it is only 900g for the underground workers and 600g for those working on top. But you receive that every day and it never fails to arrive."

"Yes," we answered.

"See, my people outside do not have the pleasure of a piece of bread every day. I know, the bread is not very good, wet and very sour, but it is bread all the same. Quite apart from the price they have to pay for a loaf, bread is in short supply and they have to queue very often, come rain or snow, for hours, sometimes days until they get bread, one loaf for each family of four. And you receive wages for your labour at the same rate as everyone else. Officers get sugar and tobacco and butter, lard or margarine. Every month, not much, but they get it. Don't they?"

We had to agree.

"So, why are you ungrateful and do not work harder than you do?"

That was it, then. He wanted more coal, probably so that he could receive a bonus.

Sub looked me straight in the eye, expecting an answer. What could I say? He was right as far as the conditions were concerned, so what sort of answer could I properly give that would not upset him? Eureka, I found one.

"Sir," I said, "what you mentioned is correct. However, there is one difference between your people outside the barbed wire and us inside, which you have not touched upon. The distinction is that your people on the outside can walk freely wherever they care to choose, and they can go home, whatever that home is. We cannot. If you care to put it that way, this is why we seem to be ungrateful."

Major Sub remained silent. After a few moments he waved his hand, and we were dismissed. The subject was never raised again.

Rumours buzzed around the camp that a transport would be put together soon so that all invalids, Category Four and camp service personnel would be repatriated. It seemed no more than reasonable because, after all, for some months Russian mine workers had begun to arrive and take over the workings. Two districts, my own included, were now run by the Russians and everything pointed towards a complete evacuation of us PoWs. By mid-March the rumours began to bear fruit. Barrack by barrack, transports began leaving, kitted out in new uniforms, for the repatriation camp near Uzlovaya. Lucky them: they would be home by Easter.

Only the Anti-Fascist activists and the camp service people stayed behind with our group to await transfer.

The inhabitants of my hut were shipped only a short distance towards Tula and assigned to a new camp where we were to be involved not in mining as such, but in the construction of a new mining complex. It was a brand new unit.

All the barrack buildings were spick and span and had never housed prisoners before. No longer were we the original one thousand bodies which had been kept together and counted and counted and counted. That group had been divided into separate units when we left Lager 388 and so it was that we now numbered just two hundred and fifty. From the camp site we walked three kilometres every day along a railway line to the new workplace. A large banner told us that the mine was being developed by the Young Pioneers and that they had pledged to complete the construction of all buildings and the sinking of the exploration shaft well, in advance of the target date set in honour of the Glorious October Revolution by the seventh of October.

The only thing wrong with this was that there were not enough Pioneers to do the job and so the good old battle cry rose once more to the skies: "Germans to the Front!" We were not, frankly, very enthused of working for the glory of both the Pioneers and the Revolution, so we did not exert ourselves unduly. Apart from that, the weather had again turned very cold, which made it difficult to lay bricks as the mortar would freeze instead of setting. Luckily for Wilfried and me, we were attached to the sawmill as we had done a similar job previously in the last camp. How much would we get paid? we asked. The answer was simple: there was no chance of earning anything.

We had absolutely no incentive to meet the norm of so many metres of slats a day. They were to be used to support plaster and to make trellises, but this was pointless because the frost prevented anyone from working on the buildings anyway.

Two months later, much to our surprise, we read in the newspaper, *The Young Komsomolsk*, that the Pioneer Brigade developing this new mine had completed its construction work and was now well on the way to meeting its pledge. Well, they certainly had completed it, on paper, but then all reports were faked so we could almost understand how the completion of a project which had not even started could be announced.

Were there any thinking people in the Soviet Union? I wondered. How long could a state live with such lies and deceits?

With the arrival of Whitsun, our small concert party laid on a show. The weather was beautiful and we were given the Sunday off. What a glorious, wonderful day! Fifty of us, myself included, were told that we would be sent home. The list of those to be repatriated, we were told, had arrived that morning from Moscow.

At long last the day for which I had been waiting so long had arrived. At first I would not believe my luck, but next morning, everyone except the lucky fifty left for work. We were called up for a final interrogation and were issued new clothing, and now the message finally got through and the world began to look rosy again. Mail had arrived as well that day, and I was one of the many who received news from home after a lull of almost two years.

We were also told that the money which had been banked in our names could not be taken out of the country, but that it could be used to buy any goods – from salami sausages to cigarettes and watches to motor bikes – which we could afford. These goods, we were told, would be on offer in the main repatriation camp and could be taken away on the train to freedom. The excitement grew.

We were called to a final roll-call and asked to have all our possessions with us, as we would soon be leaving the camp. Our Russian camp commander told us that nobody would be able to decline repatriation. If anyone wanted to remain in the Soviet Union they would have to go home first and then apply for re-entry. He reminded us to remain good anti-Fascists and tell our countrymen the truth about Russia (no fear of that, we thought).

"You are allowed to take home everything you possess, including whatever you buy, with one exception. Any lice must stay here. They are Soviet property."

Left turn, quick march to the gate. There stood our political commissar, who began to read from a list in his hand the names of those who had been told to go home. One after the other stepped forward, passed through the gate and climbed on to the waiting lorry. Forty-nine of them. My name had not been called. With tears in my eyes, I asked if he had made a mistake. But no, my name had been struck off the list at the last moment.

My world collapsed and I wept. No consoling by my comrades could stop the tears. In the afternoon my political captain called me to his office and I was seething so much that I really felt I could have killed him, given the chance.

"Sorry about the delay," he said. "I will send you home, trust me, but for the time being I still need you. You will be sent home, but with the last train."

Need me? For what? I knew this man from as far back as Yavas, but surely there could be no excuse for interfering with my going home? I was dismissed and went back to my friends. Somehow I had to overcome the disappointment, and with the help of Wilfried, who had also remained in the camp, managed to get my feet firmly back on the ground. No matter what my feelings, nothing could change the situation.

We were allowed to write home twice a month, and replies began to come through fairly regularly. It was those letters from my parents, so full of information about the improvements in life back home, which made me look forward with increasing impatience to the day when it would all be over. At least repatriation had started, even if slowly, so there was room for hope.

With the end of summer, autumn came flooding in. Normally the weather would turn cold suddenly, but this time the heavens opened and rain poured down in buckets. The administration was not one bit bothered about the soggy conditions. We had to go to the Komsomolsk Pit even though this meant that we would stand around all day doing very little.

The ground was like a bog, for our clever production target achievers had not only forgotten to lay drains, they seemed to have forgotten to order any drain pipes. I rationalised it thus: to develop a project like this needs planning and thinking, but thinking hurts and, after all the head was provided by the Lord to cover with a cap and not to think with. The impression I had so very often was that in Russia one didn't think. Leave thinking to the horses: they have larger heads!

In October the camp was closed and we had to march off. We actually went slightly closer to home, but only a few kilometres.

Unfortunately my 'last train' captain came with us. I could not lose him, and he seemed determined not to lose me.

The new camp was quite unlike any of the others which we had populated. It consisted not only of wooden sheds, but also had some army-style barrack buildings made of brick to house the guards and the camp administration. Although some of the rooms in the brick huts were unoccupied, we were directed to the standard and accustomed timber villas. The camp commandant, who received us together with his immediate staff, could have been cut from a turn-of-the-century photograph of a typical Tsarist officer. He sported a magnificent, silver grey beard that was groomed to perfection. It adorned a kind-hearted, almost benevolent looking face. His impeccable uniform was without a single blemish. A row of medal ribbons decorated the left side of his tunic. He wore long trousers, unlike the other commandants who always tried to impress upon us their military status by wearing riding breeches and boots. He had a deep and mellow voice and, all in all, was the embodiment of an officer and a gentleman.

No doubt it was his doing, but before very long a band was formed, and played in the dining hall during meal times. Whatever would there be next!

On the morning after our arrival, with one of my comrades, who had been heading a working brigade, I was appointed shift district manager.

As opposed to the previous pit, this one was thankfully dry. The method of extracting the coal was also different. The coal here was rock hard, and had to be blasted with dynamite. First a slot was cut along the entire length of the face, by a machine like a chainsaw, about fifty centimetres above the floor and two metres deep. We drilled the holes for the sticks of dynamite, but the loading and firing had to be carried out only by a Russian. The one assigned to my district was continually drunk and therefore quite incapable of carrying out his noble duties. So, as we wanted to earn some money on the way, we came to an arrangement.

He gave us the dynamite, the detonators and the fuse wire, which we buried under sand in an inconspicuous place, and we helped him with his drink problem by furnishing him, from various indirect sources, with the alcohol he craved. This made us independent and worked like a charm. All that was necessary was for him to attend the blast operation in case an inspection was carried out by the mining engineer. In time for the detonation we woke him up, led him safely to the coal face, and took him back to a quiet spot to continue with his hobby.

So far as I was concerned, there was a major drawback to the new job: I was permanently on night shift. However, I got used to it in time, and found it to be not all that bad. In contrast to the main mining camp, we were not called upon to do any inter-shift work, like unloading railway wagons, and as everyone in our, much smaller, barrack was on the same shift, our sleep was never disturbed by the comings and goings of other shift workers. My position as district 'natschalnik' entitled me to a pass allowing me to leave camp at any time to go into the mine prior to the arrival of the workforce, mainly to inspect my district and ascertain its readiness for the shift. Being able to walk alone, at my own pace and unguarded, gave me a feeling of freedom and I took full advantage of this privilege, leaving the camp whenever I wanted.

One night, when I went to the coal face, I was surprised to find that the previous shift had finished all preparations for the new hauling. The caving-in of the adjacent stretch had been done, the chain conveyor had been installed, all blast holes had been drilled and the slot cutting machine, having done its job, had been removed. Compressed air was working and all electric lines and connections were in working order. I saw a chance for doing little, but producing much!

When my shift arrived I told them of my plan. Stuff the holes with dynamite – which was available thanks to our intoxicated blast master – start the conveyor belt and chain conveyor rolling and blast the whole front (all thirty metres x three metres x two point three metres) in one shot, and let the chain conveyor do the work. The coal face would collapse over the moving chain which should scrape the heap of coal away and on to the main conveyor. "Prailna?" – good? All we had to do was to stand by, shovel the coal on to the conveyor when it became necessary to keep the black gold flowing, and to secure the ceiling from collapsing, with the help of our specialist support building crew, of course. Off went the shots, down came the coal and at the front loading point the coal arrived in abundance.

I went to see the chief engineer of the mine and informed him that District Three was in the process of delivering a major haul and that I needed all the transport I could get. He came with me to satisfy himself of the situation, smelled the imminent chance of a record-breaking shift and, never mind the other four districts and their needs for transport, redirected all available wagons and locomotives to my district. The other departments were starved of the majority of their transport facilities, but that did not matter. What was important? Produce a record, and if it is to the detriment of others that would be bad luck to them. The news that something exceptional was happening in District Three travelled fast and alerted not only the director of the mine – who made one of his rare visits underground, wherein he smiled and patted my shoulder – but also the camp.

"Gans, you are producing the chance of a lifetime to have the gods of medals and glory smile at us. Long live the Revolution which allows us to achieve such heroic deeds."

By the time the shift was over we had 'produced' one hundred and seventy-four tons of coal. This was a new national record and represented twenty-eight tons per head. When I emerged up top with my men we were greeted, yes greeted, by the sergeant of the watch, separated from all the others and led well ahead of the rest back to the camp. I could not believe my eyes. There was the band playing march music, the Old Man in his finest parade uniform complete with white tunic, all medals on display (not just the ribbons), dark blue trousers with red piping and black shoes shining like mirrors.

Next to the Commandant stood the Political Captain, my personal 'friend', and the rest of the administration in their best uniforms and lined up like organ pipes, along with whoever was available of our own people. What on earth was happening?

The Major stepped forward before we had marched over the camp threshold, first shook my hand, then embraced me and uttered words like, "Congratulations, my hero, congratulations and the nation's appreciation for breaking the national record for the production of coal in one shift by one man."

By one man? There had been seven more who worked for this, but that was how it ever was and always had been throughout history. The one in charge receives the honours. Well, I had to live with that and hoped my comrades did not bear me any grudge. Later I discovered in the best possible way that they did not.

Our silverbeard continued, "In recognition of your deed, you and your men will now be transferred to the brick building where you will be given individual rooms, one room for two people, and you, Gans, will have your own, all for yourself. Each of you will also receive two sets of brand new underwear, two white cotton shirts, socks and new uniforms as well as a white tunic and an extra pair of shoes, and you will sit in the dining room at a special table where a batman will serve you. You will not queue for your food. Soap is available on request, the bath is available at all times and so is the hairdresser, who has been instructed to come to your quarters, if you so wish. A special pass will be issued so that you can leave the camp and walk about at your leisure."

We were absolutely flabbergasted, but this was not Shakespeare's *Much Ado About Nothing*. It was real, a spectacle, theatre of the highest order. And we played the leading part in all that.

The following morning, when we came up at the end of our shift, we saw as we stepped out of the lift that a board had been erected by the camp gate commemorating my name, the achievement, the date and, in capital letters, the words 'STACHANOVSKI ACTIVIST' and underneath, 'GENNEKOVSKI ACTIVIST'. Now what was all that about? I had never heard of a man called 'Gennekov'. Our camp Anti-fascist, yes he was still with us, then informed me that a few days before, in East Germany, a miner by the name of Hennecke had announced that he would break all coal production records in honour of some God-knows-what special occasion, had gone down the mine and emerged victorious. Every good worker in the DDR (German Democratic Republic), which had been proclaimed shortly before, was now striving to follow his great example and get their name on the honours board. It nearly made one sick, this farce. However, we enjoyed our new status to the full and could only laugh each time our waiter, also dressed in a white jacket, brought a tray and served us with our wooden dishes of sauerkraut soup and kasha and a piece of heavy, wet, sour bread.

Time passes, as the saying goes, until we arrived at the beginning of 1949, which was destined to be my last year in Russia. Right after 'breakfast' one morning I was summoned to the Major's office, to be presented to a woman in uniform. She was small, plump, exceedingly buxom and to my mind, even after so long away from my kind of civilisation, extraordinarily ugly. She was dressed in a short skirt that was a size too small and a tunic that was about to be split asunder by her massive bust. This unlovely person had done her best to cover up her misshapen face with a good half-pound of powder and rouge. She had painted her massive lips to make them look even larger. Around her clung an odour which suggested that she had been scrummaging around at a perfume factory in a bin marked 'unsuitable for humans'.

It was immediately clear that the Major shared my dislike for her, judging by the expression on his face. It would take at least a fortnight to give the office an airing.

"You are the Stachanovski Activist who broke the record?" she declared in a voice like a snarling crocodile. "I am pleased to meet such an ardent defender of peace, and a great anti-fascist. Tell me, could you do it again and break your own record? The Day of the Red Army is forthcoming on the twenty-fourth of January and I want to present our great leader General Stalin with a gift of memorable value."

SHE wanted to present him! What about me and my fellow slaves? Could we really refuse to perform a second miracle which might help her gain promotion from First Lieutenant to Captain? And what would be our fate if we accepted the challenge – and then failed?

I decided that we were in no position to turn her down so I put as bold a face on it as I could.

"Why not?" I told her. "I think it can be done, provided the conditions underground are right."

"Leave that to me. Whatever you need, I will see to it."

So I explained that what I wanted was exactly the state of preparation which had existed when my record-breaking shift had come on duty. She must have been incredibly keen, for on the twenty-third of January I was informed that everything had been attended to.

As usual, I went down the mine about half an hour before my shift came on to start work. There was an eerie silence. From my district all the way back to the lift, the mine's entire transport facilities were lined up, one train behind the other, very effectively bringing the pit to a complete standstill. Until the first load came from my district and the rail points were freed of the locomotives parked right over them, nothing anywhere could move. My district was silent, too.

There was nobody at the loading apron, no light and no hissing of compressed air. My lamp lit the path to the rear, where I could hear faintly the timber breaking under the strain of sand released by the caving-in of the previous workings. I sensed disaster.

The chain conveyor was lying in pieces, waiting to be assembled. No electrical power supply seemed to be working, the drive of the main conveyor had been moved forward, but the belt itself had not been installed. The coal face in all its black glory stood there solidly with no blast holes drilled. One thing was sure: this coal would not contribute to the glory of the Red Army Day and that of my aspiring little Miss First Lieutenant.

I went back up to the surface and went to see the pit director, who was lying on his standard-issue leather sofa, all dressed in his parade uniform of white tunic, medals and black trousers with yellow piping. Also, to my disgust, he was snoring. I woke him and explained the extent of my investigation. He jumped up as though he had been stung by a scorpion, rushed to the communicating door into the office of the chief engineer. He, too, was expecting another hour of glory, being dressed for the occasion – and sound asleep on his sofa. Neither man would believe my story and followed me like tigers, dressed in all their finery, down and to the head of my district. There was no disputing the truth of what they saw, but one boss started to blame the other and they both stormed back to the top.

The immediate problem was how to disentangle the spaghetti of the underground railway system. It was rather like a game of solitaire played with a child's model railway. If they moved the first train, they would free the head of the track from trucks but this would not be enough to make it possible to recycle the loaded trucks when they arrived from my district. They could not continue to the other districts after the trucks were discharged because their way would be blocked by other trains. The only solution was to send all the empty trucks to the surface, where they would be turned around and sent back to the bottom once there was room. Only after a very elaborate recycling of the entire rolling stock, which would take hours, was there a chance that any coal at all could be produced, let alone a record-breaking quantity. All facilities of the mine had been arranged to serve my district which, for the simplest of reasons, was unable to perform.

My shift arrived, I explained the situation, we went a few metres back and sat in a recess, huddled together to keep warm. We then settled down for a good eight hours' rest.

"Nje rabota, towaritsh" – No working, comrade.

Morning arrived and we went up to clock-off shift. With a guard of honour we were led straight back to the camp. All the arrangements were as before, with band, music, major, commissar and the Iron Maiden. She smiled at me and, almost whispered, from excitement, the words, "Skolko, Gans?" – How much, Gans?

There was only one possible answer.

"Nje huya, nje gramma," I said. Not a bloody gram.

Her face turned ashen, the Major almost lost his balance.

"Why, you bastard, why?"

I explained that no preparations had been made and the whole thing had turned sour, whereupon there issued from her mouth the most insulting accusations imaginable interspersed with swearwords worthy of a docker after dropping a two ton crate on his big toe.

Having been a guest of the Soviet Union for over four years, I was not totally surprised. Russian is probably the one language which embraces the most vile swearwords of all the others. These expressions were used by all and sundry irrespective of their upbringing, at least during my experience. If one removed all the swearwords from a heated conversation, nothing would be left of any relevance to the subject in question.

Madam blew her top. She let me know that to her mind I had been shown up to be not only a fascist, but a warmonger, a war criminal, a son of a bitch and a whore, and only worthy to be crushed under a sledge hammer. Unfortunately she could not do this, but she would see that I was sent to a penal company. Luckily for me, this was also something she could not do. She was on firmer ground when she ranted on and stated that my men and I would immediately lose all our privileges. I would lose my job, too. Back you go, back to work at the coal face.

And so it was. We marched off, not back to our single rooms, but to the communal wooden shed. We had to return our double rations of underwear, the white tunic, the special passes and the surplus soap. No more would we sit at the table to be served, but would queue like everyone else. And indignity of indignity, when we went to the barber it would be at the time that we were told to go, and not when we chose. All that remained of our glory was the board with our names that showed me as 'Stachanovski Activist'. Nobody could take that away from me.

The painted harridan took off. Shortly afterwards I was called to the Major, whom I found sitting at his desk, a broken man. How could I do that to him? Had he not been good to us, and gentle? And now this humiliation. Worse still, the silly moo had sent a telegram that morning to Moscow informing the authorities that the record had been broken again in honour of the Day of the Red Army, the twenty-fourth of January. I could not help thinking how remarkably naïve it was of the Major to have expected anything else. After all, he must have known how records are made in Russia and that chickens were often counted even if they did not hatch. Sadly, two days later the good old fool was replaced.

We spent only one more month in that camp. Nothing more was said about the abortive record breaking affair which seemed to have been forgotten, though one suspects that it was never forgiven. My Political Captain did not tell me whether or not there were any further repercussions.

PROMOTION BRINGS A MIXED BLESSING

The day came when we clambered on to lorries en route for yet another camp. This time we were headed for Uzlovaya. I, for one, viewed this move with only one feeling: good riddance to a hateful place and a loathsome experience. So far as I was concerned, the very best of luck to Stachanov and Hennecke, wherever they were. Long may they keep up the good work for the Workers' Paradise, but heaven help me never to go down a mine again.

It had been three years since I first came across Uzlovaya, remembered for the days of liberated ox tongues, rabbits and buckwheat. I was actually quite looking forward to seeing the old place again, but I never learn! We were taken instead to a much larger camp than the one I knew, capable of holding up to three thousand detainees at any one time. When we arrived there were already a few hundred soldiers still working the local coal mine. Thankfully we were not forced to go down, but having reached such an advanced position in the pits, and to satisfy my curiosity, I volunteered for an inspection-cum-sightseeing tour.

It was quite remarkable that nobody expected me to work in earnest, because my fame as a Stachanovski Activist had preceded me. The bush drums work fast and far in the mining community!

The mine into which I was going to descend was long established. As opposed to those with which I was familiar, this one had coal seams as high as four metres in places. Tunnels extended from the lift shaft like tentacles in all directions, and everywhere there was water. I thought that I had experienced water during my first coal encounter, but this was not just water: it was the Great Flood in its infancy. Pure rain from the roof, running water from the walls and streams on the floor. The miners had to work the face from scaffolding in order to reach the height and were clad in trousers alone. It was not really cold, because the ventilation was not forced, but was by natural draught. Looking into these huge caverns and seeing people slaving away, and clinging to a web of different structures was like watching a scene from Dante's Inferno. I was glad to be allowed not to work in such appalling conditions. Everything I encountered down there left an everlasting impression on me.

By the end of the week I was called to my commissar captain.

"Gans, as you will have guessed, this is the central repatriation camp. During the next months many PoWs will pass through this camp to be sent home, but not before we have separated the good guys from the bad guys – the war criminals from the decent soldiers."

"What is a war criminal, Captain?" I asked.

"Anybody who has perpetrated a crime, such as stolen state property, damaged the people's woods and hedgerows, slaughtered the people's livestock and misbehaved in general towards the population of the occupied areas."

What a list of 'crimes'. If he ever found out that I had ripped off some twigs from a bush for camouflage or killed a pig so my men and I could eat, I would never reach home again, I thought. But why was he telling me all this? The answer nearly toppled me over.

"Gans, from now on you are in charge of this camp. I put you above all inhabitants. I need you to organise the near chaos I am expecting once the transports arrive. Get yourself a decent interpreter. Now follow me."

He went down the corridor, opened the last door and asked me to step inside.

"This is your office. The next room is for your interpreter. Whenever I need to talk to you, I'll call. Ponial? - understood?" And with that he left me to my own devices.

The room was large, three metres by four metres, right across the width of the building. It contained a writing desk with an armchair, and a few chairs around a table on which rested a chess board. One window overlooked the parade ground, the other faced the main gate and guard house. I was so shattered by my translation from working hand to administrator that I slumped into my armchair and felt obliged to take a deep breath. Surely, this was a a total Alice in Wonderland situation, if ever there was one!

How could I possibly do what he expected of me unless he spelled out exactly what the job entailed and how I was to go about it. What authority did I have, and over whom? I had no staff, so was I supposed to select a suitable team to work for me? Experience had taught me that it was quite in order to formulate the questions, but that I had better not ask this particular mentor for any answers. I would just have to get on with the job as best as I could.

An announcement appeared on the information board, in Russian and in German, informing the astounded populace of the appointment and telling everyone that if anyone had anything of importance to say about camp life they were to report to me.

I decided to take the bull by the horns and find out what I could about the way things were organised, so I went off on a round of the camp, introducing myself to the assorted camp service chiefs and invited them, together with the seniors in charge of individual barracks, to a chat session. There I divided up the responsibilities, leaving in charge those who already had their own departments. I impressed upon everyone that the camp was to be kept immaculately clean. I told them that I was not going to interfere with the way they performed their duties. However, I wished to be informed immediately of any changes in personnel due to repatriation and that any superior about to leave the camp was expected to install his successor.

I let it be known that each Monday morning I wished to receive a verbal report about the state of affairs of each barrack, the kitchen and the general camp service.

Off they all went and I made my first rounds in order to familiarise myself with the camp, of which I then knew little, and to search for an interpreter. There were several candidates for this exuberant position and I settled in the end for a young, distinguished-looking former sergeant. That he had belonged to the Waffen SS did not matter an iota. Like many thousands of conscripts within that division, he had had no say about which unit he was to join. In any case, my war service had taught me that the Waffen SS was identical to any other army unit, be it artillery, panzer, infantry, engineers and so on. To be on the safe side, though, I did not tell my captain about these finer points of military hierarchy.

Everyday the captain came over to play a game of chess and discuss general matters, but I soon realised that each time he talked about one specific aspect of the camp and its inhabitants. I always called on my interpreter to help, and the clever political commissar could never understand why I had to go through an interpreter on those occasions. After all, could he not talk amicably when we were playing chess? He never found the solution to this niggling question. The simple reason was that whilst I had understood most of what was being translated, the process gave me time to formulate my answer, which thus could appear to be quite 'spontaneous' immediately after the interpreter had finished.

During the ensuing weeks small transports would arrive in the camp and be registered, and every day small groups left the camp. One or two of those who left the camp returned a few days later, but the rest were never seen again. Because this puzzled me, I began questioning the returnees. The whole thing was mysterious, to say the least.

The more I delved into what was going on the more I was convinced that those who came back had been decoys. Each of them told the same story. They were not necessarily sent to the same camp, but to different small ones which had been set up for a special purpose. Each camp had a 'court' where PoWs were 'tried' for 'war crimes' of the type about which the captain had spoken. In order to disguise this activity, some PoWs in whom the Russians were not really interested, were added to each batch of suspects and returned as unwanted. In next to no time I got the complete picture of the network of courts, which imposed the standard sentence on those found guilty – of twenty-five years in a labour camp. I put together a list detailing such matters as the persons presiding at those courts, as well as the names, ranks and general attitude of the panel members towards their prey.

When I was convinced that I was on the right track, I ordered that each time a new transport arrived its members were to be housed together in one barrack and were registered by us before the Russians could get hold of them. I then called the individual men to my office and questioned them about their real names, army or SS units and their precise involvement during the War, such as fighting partisans. After I had explained the reason for the grilling, I impressed upon them that I could only help if they made a full and honest disclosure to me. After they had told me everything that I wanted to know, I was able to tell them about the fate that possibly lay in wait. I was able to prepare many for being 'processed' at a given camp by telling them who would be questioning them, together with the particular speciality of the court. Based on the information I had drawn together, I proceeded to suggest how they should conduct their interrogation, what subjects to avoid, if possible, as well as how to go about finding a credible explanation that would destroy the accusation.

Over the weeks and months that followed my 'day of enlightenment' I was busy trying to protect as many of my fellow countrymen from a twenty-five year sentence as possible. The captain, who must have suspected something, asked me only once why I saw all the newcomers in my office. My answer was simple. Having been put in charge of the camp, I wanted to make sure we had no troublemakers among us. Where I sensed even minimal unrest, I could interfere and stop the rot in its infancy. He was delighted that I took my job so seriously!

Many of those whom I was able to warn either came back from their outing, or were passed on to other release camps and so got home safely. I knew that I was gambling, even with my own chance for repatriation, but good fortune coupled, I am convinced, with the protection of my political commissar, made it possible to conduct the undercover rescue operation effectively and securely.

Although my camp was the central one in the repatriation process, there were other collecting camps around us. These were administered by the Russian HQ of the district and it was from those that the first groups of any size were put together and sent on their way. The evacuation of camps began operating in earnest and by August of 1949, one transport after the other began to roll to the west. My camp, on the other hand, was kept up to strength during all this time, mainly because of the 'war criminal' trials.

The world was to learn some two years later that, after 1949 the Russians had detained twenty-five thousand German soldiers branded as war criminals, and shipped them to Siberia. They were released, thanks to the intervention of Konrad Adenauer of West Germany, in 1952. Of course not every one of those went through my camp.

Every evening, from the beginning of September, my political commissar received a list of those who were to be released. He would call me as soon as the list arrived and read out the names in my presence, just in case I wanted to tip off a friend ahead of the good news being published. Naturally, each time I hoped to hear my own name, but there was no chance.

"I will get you home, but not until the last transport," he would say, reminding me that he had made this promise to me. I was convinced that he had a finger in the pie and made sure he could hang on to me as long as possible. All right, I thought, so long as he keeps his word the days must be numbered.

Wilfried and Heinz, who had been with me for so long, departed with my wishes for a speedy return and carrying letters to my parents, with the request that they look them up and give them my personal greetings. Once they had gone I felt particularly lonely and submerged myself in the task of keeping the rest of the inmates contented.

No sooner did one transport leave than new arrivals would fill the barracks again. Fewer and fewer were required to make their way to the court camps and the time eventually arrived when the camp was no more than a transit station for the train.

Every evening when the repatriation list arrived became increasingly frustrating for me. We would sit, as always, in the captain's office, the list would be read out and I would suffer another bout of disappointment. I got really angry with him on one occasion when he had the total lack of sensitivity to say to me, "See, Gans, your God won't help you to get home. It is Stalin who decrees who can leave and when."

The remark was so silly that I had a shot at getting him off the subject altogether by starting a conversation about religion, God and faith. I could see that he was strangely interested. Here was something to debate, and he liked debating. With the help of the interpreter, my Russian not being up to forcefully debating such an intricate topic, we argued back and forth until I asked him to risk being convinced that, far from being an atheist, he might really believe in God. Our parry and thrust went something like this...

"Do you believe that our life is controlled by something yet unknown to us?"

"Naturally, but our scientists will come up with an answer."

"Do you believe that our solar system and our galaxy, and all the other galaxies and stars are governed by an inexplicable force which no scientist has been able to discover or even vaguely describe?"

"We are searching for it and know that magnetism and changes in the cosmic system have something to do with it, but our researchers and physicists will provide the answer. There is an explanation for everything that is related to mathematics and physics."

"So, you do not know. Nobody knows. Nobody can explain. And because it is impossible to provide an acceptable answer, for thousands of years the human race has tried to give this inexplicable something a name; has believed in this unknown force which controls our lives and what we grow, what we create, what we cannot touch, and still believes in it. Even those who think they are atheists. In order to have something tangible, something real, though unreal at the same time, those who have been created by high force have given it a name. They call it Buddha, Shinto, God. Man has at times prayed even to the sun and the moon. All these objects of faith were considered at the time to be the closest that man could conceive to the mighty, the Almighty, who is controlling us and who we are and what we are. Do you believe in this inexplicable force which is chased by scientists and spiritual leaders alike, though none have even a glimmer of what they are looking for, because they do not know whether it can be found at all?"

I realised that I was sharing my innermost thoughts, something I had little expected to do with someone who was my captor, but in the spirit of our debate I thought it perfectly valid to do so. When I stopped to draw breath, I expected an answer, but certainly not what came.

"Yes, I do believe in this inexplicable something, as you call it," said my Political Commissar.

What else was there for me to say, except to draw the obvious conclusion.

"If you believe in that which is unknown to any of us, yet is greater than our puny brains can comprehend, you believe in a god of some description, if not in God. You can be many things, but you are not an atheist."

He looked at me without saying a word, no doubt surprised at the turn our debate had taken. I could see that his mind was working furiously and, indeed, he seemed by his very expression to be weighing his own feelings on the subject. He might have fallen back on Communist dogma in which he, as the Political Commissar, was steeped, but he did not. Whether or not I managed to convince him that my view was right, is not important. However, I firmly believe that he took a step on the dangerous path of thinking for himself.

A few days later, at the beginning of December, I sat listening to my captain droning on through yet another long list of names for repatriation. I forget what I was thinking about at the time, but I do know that my attention was definitely wandering. Something registered in the middle of his monotonous flow and I woke up with a start. My own name had been read out. I interrupted and asked him to go back a few names and start reading again. And again, there it was. My own name rang out into my ears. I jumped up and said, "That's it. It is me. From now on, Captain, I am a free man."

"Forget it," he replied. "The deal was that I would get you home on the last train. I still need you until the whole repatriation business is finished."

"It is finished, Captain. I am going home, now," I retorted, whereupon I left the room, went to my bunk and started packing.

The following morning the captain came to my office and told me that he had been overruled. He had asked Moscow whether I could be delayed, but was told that the trainload being put together would bring the repatriation of German PoWs to an end. Consequently, that was that. However, not only would he make the trip to see us home safely, but in recognition of my assistance I would be in charge of the German contingent. That was an honour I could have done without.

Two days later the train drew in. It may not have been luxury accommodation, but it was infinitely superior to anything I had experienced in Russia. For instance, the wagons were equipped with two double plank-beds at either end of the truck, each accommodating a maximum of sixteen PoWs. In the rest of the space was a table, some chairs and a stove for keeping the whole rolling villa nice and warm despite the chilly winter weather.

Before boarding we were paid our accumulated 'savings' and invited to spend them in the bazaar which had been arranged in the camp and through which we had to go to reach the train. Everything imaginable was on show: wristwatches, pocket watches, motorcycles, foodstuffs of all kind, cigarettes and handicrafts. Whoever had roubles had to spend them as we were not allowed to take out any money. I had only a few hundred and thought that the best bet for me would be cigarettes and smoked salami which might come in handy for bartering, if the need arose. Somewhere on my travels I had acquired a wooden sort of suitcase, complete with lock, in place of a rucksack or satchel and into this went my goodies.

Off we went to the loading platform. I stayed behind overseeing the boarding process, and selected a wagon in the middle of the train which was only occupied by thirty men, instead of the average thirty-six. The locomotive blew its whistle, and slowly we pulled out of Uzlovaya. When I looked out of the car and back to the station there was, indeed, no other train left in the sidings.

On the eighteenth of December we arrived in Brest-Litovsk, the last large station on Russian soil. Once it had been Polish, but was annexed by the Soviet Union at the outbreak of hostilities in 1939.

I GET HOME AT LAST

There were six days to Christmas, which should surely have been enough time to reach home for the festival, but when the train was shunted on to one of the many lines of this enormous marshalling yard, I was shocked to see it crammed with transport trains just like ours. There were close on forty waiting to be given final clearance by the Russians. If we had to wait our turn there would be no chance of seeing our families even for the New Year. But this was a time for optimism, I told myself. Much could happen in six days and I hoped that the authorities would deal with matters in hand speedily.

So we waited, and strolled among the other groups which were all impatient to get going again. Slowly, much too slowly, one train after the other left. Why all the delay? I noticed that, as each train was emptied, all its occupants had to pass right through a couple of barracks close by the line. I went up to one of the men who had gone through this procedure and asked for details. Firstly, it seemed, everyone undressed and passed through a delousing station. Secondly everyone was called up by name to a cubicle where a Russian officer sat with the man's personal file and conducted a last minute inquisition by going meticulously through every detail recorded during earlier interrogations. Perhaps this was to see whether one of the answers he now received might be justified in retaining the poor devil on Soviet soil and sending him to Siberia instead of Germany.

I learned that there had been occasions where PoWs had been separated from their comrades and led away to yet another hut, but could not establish whether they had been able to rejoin their repat transport again.

The closer it got to Christmas Eve the more impatient we became. Nobody seemed to pay any attention to our train. Then Christmas Eve arrived and we had no option but to make the best of our situation. We sat in our mobile abode and sang Christmas carols and songs. Someone found some timber somewhere in the yard and was able to construct a crude Christmas tree. This was then decorated with stars and figurines cut out from meat tins, and candles which burned all night, in silent vigil, so to speak.

We were all truly despondent, seeing all the other trains pull out of the yard, their passengers laughing and singing and looking forward to their last few days in captivity. Ours was certainly the last to leave Soviet soil, for since we had arrived no further trains joined on behind. So once again we were the last of the many.

It was the day after Christmas when, early in the morning, things began to get going. We were told to disembark, lined up, called up and marched with lifting spirits to the final cleansing, in the true sense of the word. Delousing over, my turn came to enter the interrogation booth. A first lieutenant conducted the questioning.

He opened my file, asked my name and rank, and passed on to general questions about my army career. Next he wanted to know how I felt about my years in Russia, the kind of treatment I had received, whether I had any complaints, and whether I bore the Soviet Union any grudge.

I told him openly and honestly what I thought, much as I have set down here. He looked across the table, smiled and suddenly said, "Had you ever been fighting partisans?"

So far, I had always made a point of being straight in my replies, but I wondered how I should answer this.

Did the records show anything about my wartime engagements in Russia? Just in case, I decided to be open about these, too. As I had not been subjected to a trial in the last camp, I was convinced that the correct answer to that question could not do me any harm.

"Yes, I fought partisans up and down the Eastern Front, from southern Lithuania to the Ukraine, last time near Bialistok and a place by the name of Eristovka," I told him.

He looked into my eyes, smiled and said, "Thank you. You are telling the truth. I wish you a good journey home."

The weight of sheer relief on hearing these words must have been equivalent to at least the tonnage of coal which earned me the title of Stachanovski Activist – and I bet that was in my file too.

We reboarded our train and went off into a beautiful winter morning. Now we were going home the clatter of the wheels made magical music, while the noise of the rushing wind was a constant reminder that every minute took us closer to our loved ones.

Whenever we stopped, and this happened quite often to let regular trains pass, men, women and even children approached us to barter items of food so that during the following three days I managed to change all my cigarettes for butter or sausages or milk. I enjoyed the whole journey. Even at night the excitement kept me from sleep most of the time.

It seemed as though we were meant to remember the Russian reliance on head-counting even on this part of our trip. I recall that during one of our stops, at a small Polish railway station, we all alighted and mixed with the locals, laughing together and chatting with the considerable aid of sign language. The call came to rejoin the train, and everyone rushed back to their trucks. The train pulled out, but came to a halt in a siding a short while later. One of the carriages was two men short, it turned out. Out we all got again, were lined up and counted. Right enough, we were two 'dsheluwicki' (humans) short. What now? I could see the Russian escort, headed by our captain, holding an emergency conference. So far as they were concerned, this was a serious situation. They had to deliver the precise number of bodies to Frankfurt that had boarded the train originally and there was no chance this time to find two additional prisoners to make up the numbers.

Just then the regular Moscow to Frankfurt Express rattled past and there, on the platform of the last carriage, were our two runaways attired in the trousers and white vests they had been wearing when they missed reboarding with the rest of us. They waved and grinned and shouted, "See you in Frankfurt!" And that is what happened – we next saw them on the Frankfurt station platform. All they got for their experience was a good, but friendly, dressing down from the authority which could now relax because the two lost sheep had been found.

Over the border into Germany we went, and out of the land where, since 1917, milk and honey were supposed to have flowed but in fact had not reached the people of The Glorious Motherland.

As we crossed the bridge over the River Oder, we let out a cheer. Not long after this, the train had to stop, and a little later edged slowly into the station. Who were these children and women coming up to the side of the train? Had they come to welcome us? No, they were beggars, imploring us, the deprived PoWs, to give them bread or anything else to eat. What kind of fatherland was this? The war had been over for four years and seven months, yet the country could not feed its people? This was quite a shock, getting such a reception so soon after reaching home. I emptied my box and gave away everything edible that I had. After all, I would get fed shortly. How long did these poor souls have to go without food?

The train stopped briefly at the Frankfurt/Oder Station. Then, a few kilometres further down the line, it came to its final rest. We had reached our destination, the repatriation camp. You should have seen the rush of two thousand released soldiers leaving the train. Out and away, as quickly as possible, was the only thing everyone had on his mind. Helpers from the camp were waiting and put some order into the chaos of jubilant ex-PoWs. My captain wanted to chase some of us back to the train to do some clearing up and cleaning, but without success. All he encountered were the camp officials who resisted all interference and told him in no uncertain terms, among the roar of the crowd, "You have no jurisdiction over these men any longer. Go home, where you came from!"

Poor captain, you will have to do the cleaning yourself!

In camp we were divided into two main divisions, one group to stay in the DDR (East Germany), the other to go to Berlin or West Germany.

There we had our first good meal during all that time of our prolonged absence from home. I will never forget the delicious taste of the green french bean hotpot, cooked with ribs of lamb. One of my favourite dishes anyway. I could not get enough of it and ate and ate and ate, it seemed for hours.

Volunteers were called for who could write Russian and I joined the small band who stepped forward. We were asked to fill out the official release papers, in two languages, and the release passes. By coincidence I was given my own name to deal with. What a pleasure to see, before all the others did, my name on that grotty, yet invaluable, piece of paper. I have cherished it ever since.

Anyone wanting to telephone home had to put their name down. My name was called out over the loudspeaker system during the afternoon and I recall how my hands were trembling when I held the handset and, for the first time after all those years, heard the voices of my parents. I took good care, though, to make my voice as clear as possible, without any emotion. This was one time when the words alone were most important.

"I am back. See you tomorrow."

The next morning, when we went to board the train I found that it was so old as to be nearly decrepit, of the pre-war, single compartment, wooden bench, third-class variety. Normally meant to accommodate eight passengers, each compartment was crammed with ex-soldiers almost sitting and standing on top of one another. Never mind that though; even if we had been suspended in mid-air we would have put up with any inconvenience just to make sure that we reached freedom.

I was particularly lucky. I managed to secure a window seat. Off we went.

A thought crossed my mind. How many people would there be on the platform to meet this last trainload of PoWs? I was aware that our names had been broadcast, because since the beginning of November there had been announcements on the radio throughout the night giving the names of those fortunate ones who were to be released the following day. The telephones of those who had been waiting for so long for the return of their loved ones would not stop ringing all night if their son or husband had had his name read out. Everyone in town must have been sitting by the radio and listing to the broadcasts, which came every hour on the hour.

How would I recognise my parents among the crowd which would be drawn to the station to greet us? How would I find them, just two people among the thousands pushing each other along the side of the train? After all, there were fifteen hundred of us so, if only one relative turned up for each, there would be fifteen hundred of them! But surely there would be two, or even three, for each PoW so at least four thousand and five hundred people could be waiting. I knew that it was a large platform, for I had departed from it several times to return to the Eastern Front during the War. The last time had been in February 1945.

The train pulled in slowly to the Ostbahnhof. I could not believe how many people were on the platform to meet us. One could tell they were drawn from all walks of life, from East Berlin and West Berlin and from any town and hamlet in reach of what had, for so long, been the capital of all Germany, but was now called by the Communists, controlling part of the country, their very own capital. West Berlin at that time was an enclave surrounded by a land which had still to live under the jackboot of the Soviet Union with a government of Soviet lackeys. Shut away as we had been, we believed that this was all that remained of our defeated country and did not know that through the corridor leading westwards out of Berlin lay the other, the free, half of Germany.

The platform party was full of joy and expectation as the train came to a rest, but their faces betrayed the physical and mental suffering of the last eleven years. Although currency reform in the West was barely one year old, it was possible to tell by their fuller faces as well as their greater relaxation, quite apart from their clothing, those now living in the capitalist region. The rest were obviously living in the 'Free' People's Republic of the DDR.

Among that great throng were men and women holding boards in their hands, or carried on sticks, with photographs pinned to them with the words "Have you seen...?" plus the name and year in which the last sign of life had been received. Those poor souls had been going to the Ostbahnhof every day and every night to meet the trains since repatriation began in November. They had asked whoever they thought could give them the answer. With the arrival of the train on which I had travelled many, many of them would have their hopes finally shattered. There might be another train one day, but God only knew when that would be. Perhaps there was a glimmer of hope that the ones for whom they were waiting might turn up one day, but they really knew so little about what was happening two thousand kilometres to the east, or how any of us had fared since being taken prisoner.

I leaned out of the window as far as I could to scan the mass of people, hoping to get an early glimpse of my parents – and to my total amazement I saw them standing there. No matter that it was a bleak, miserable winter day; they beamed a ray of light right into my heart. I recognised them straight away. I had probably changed immensely over the years but there was no mistaking my father, in the same old hat and tweed coat he had worn when I last waved him goodbye and next to him was my mother, wearing the same camel coat with the fox fur collar.

My dream had come true. During the final hours of the dying year, and on the last train to Berlin, I had truly come home at last.